Selections

From Classic and Modern English Literature

Previously published by Georgian Press

Clare West

CAMBRIDGE UNIVERSITY PRESS
Cambridge, New York, Melbourne, Madrid, Cape Town, Singapore,
São Paulo, Delhi, Dubai, Tokyo, Mexico City

Cambridge University Press
The Edinburgh Building, Cambridge CB2 8RU, UK

www.cambridge.org
Information on this title: www.cambridge.org/9780521140812 (without key)
                          www.cambridge.org/9780521140836 (with key)

First published by Georgian Press (Jersey) Limited 1994
Reprinted and published by Cambridge University Press 2010 (twice)

Printed in the United Kingdom by Latimer Trend

A catalogue record for this publication is available from the British Library

ISBN 978-0-521-14081-2 Paperback without key
ISBN 978-0-521-14083-6 Paperback with key

Produced by AMR Design Ltd (www.amrdesign.com)

Cover image: © graficart.net/Alamy

CONTENTS

The Key begins on page 129 of the With Key edition.

Acknowledgements

The authors and publishers acknowledge the following sources of copyright material and are grateful for the permissions granted. While every effort has been made, it has not always been possible to identify the sources of all the material used, or to trace all copyright holders. If any omissions are brought to our notice we will be happy to include the appropriate acknowledgement on reprinting.

Agatha Christie: the extract from *4.50 from Paddington*. By permission of Aitken & Stone Limited. Copyright © Agatha Christie Limited 1957.

Daphne du Maurier: the extract from *Rebecca*. By permission of Curtis Brown Limited, London on behalf of the Estate of Daphne du Maurier. Copyright © 1938 by Daphne du Maurier Browning.

Gerald Durrell: the extract from *My Family and Other Animals*. By permission of Harper Collins Publishers Limited.

E. M. Forster: the extract from *Where Angels Fear to Tread*. By permission of King's College, Cambridge and The Society of Authors as the literary representatives of the E. M. Forster Estate.

William Golding: the extract from *Lord of the Flies*. By permission of Faber and Faber Limited.

Graham Greene: the extract from *The Third Man*. By permission of David Higham Associates and William Heinemann.

Ernest Hemingway: the extract from *A Farewell to Arms*. By permission of Jonathan Cape Limited on behalf of the Estate of Ernest Hemingway.

P. D. James: the extract from *The Skull Beneath the Skin*. By permission of Faber and Faber Limited.

George Orwell: the extract from *Down and Out in Paris and London*. By permission of Martin Secker & Warburg Limited on behalf of the Estate of the late Sonia Brownell Orwell.

Evelyn Waugh: the extract from *Brideshead Revisited*. By permission of the Peters Fraser & Dunlop Group Limited.

John Wyndham: the extract from *The Day of the Triffids*. Copyright © John Wyndham, 1951. By permission of Michael Joseph Limited.

Photographs

CSU Archive/Everett/Rex Features: page 91.

Getty Images: pages 7, 11, 15, 19, 23, 27, 31, 35, 39, 43, 47, 51, 55, 59 (Popperfoto/Getty Images), 63, 67, 71, 75, 83, 87, 95, 99, 103, 119, 123.

Mirrorpix: page 107.

News (UK) Ltd/Rex Features: page 115.

© Pictorial Press Ltd/Alamy: page 79.

Sipa Press/Rex Features: page 111.

Many thanks to John Urling Clark who did the photographic research.

INTRODUCTION

Selections contains thirty extracts from classic works in the English language. These span three centuries of literary achievement, from Daniel Defoe, who was born in 1660 and wrote what many consider to be the first English novel, to P. D. James, the current 'Queen of Crime', writing in the last years of the twentieth century. This book is an introduction to the best of English literature. I hope that the texts chosen will not only be of interest in themselves, but will also encourage students to read other works by these authors.

The texts

These are unsimplified and have been carefully selected for level, so that intermediate to upper-intermediate students, or those preparing for the Cambridge First Certificate or the IGCSE in ESL or Literature, will be able to understand them, with the help of the notes and exercises. The devices • • • or • • • • • are used occasionally to indicate where a few words or lines have been omitted.

The extracts are presented in the chronological order in which they were originally published in book form. This gives an interesting overview of the way the English language has developed in the last three hundred years. However, units may be studied in any order.

Biographical details

Each unit starts with a biographical sketch of the author, outlining his or her literary significance, with suggestions for further reading. There follows an introduction to the text. Careful reading of this page, and the extract itself, could be done as homework to prepare for the lesson.

Notes

The notes immediately following the text are intended to clarify, in language suitable for the reader's level, difficult vocabulary, structures or usage. Any ungrammatical or old-fashioned expressions are always commented on here, or in the exercises. Only the meaning of the word or expression as it is used in the text is given.

Comprehension exercises

The comprehension exercises are designed to check the reader's global understanding and to help him or her to appreciate the finer details of the text, which may not be apparent on the first reading. There is also a short preliminary exercise to check understanding of the author's biographical details.

Discussion and role-play

Discussion questions use elements of the text as a starting point, but tend to encompass wider themes, to encourage free expression of ideas. Seventeen of the units also have a role-play section, which provides extended oral practice in realistic everyday situations.

There is a short Further Discussion section at the back of the book, where students are asked to compare units, writers and writing styles.

Extension exercises

The extension exercises have two aims: to draw students' attention to important areas of syntax and lexis in the text, and to give extended practice in using them. These areas have been selected for their relevance to FCE preparation. The example word, phrase or sentence which begins each exercise always comes directly from the text.

A variety of exercise types has been used, to maintain reader interest and to reflect the different examination tasks. No specific structural rules are given: students are advised to consult *Practical English Usage, English Grammar in Use* or *Recycling Your English* if they are in doubt.

Composition work

The composition section in each unit provides suitable homework or follow-up tasks, within the FCE word limit. These questions cover all the main types of composition set in Paper 2 of the revised FCE, although the emphasis is naturally on narrative, descriptive and discursive writing.

Index

Teachers and students can refer to the Index on page 128 to check where a particular structure or vocabulary area is dealt with.

A **With Key** edition of *Selections* is available.

I very much hope that teachers and students will enjoy *Selections* and will feel inspired to explore English literature further.

Clare West, 1997

1

DANIEL DEFOE

1660 – 1731

Daniel Defoe was born in London, the son of a butcher. As a salesman of tights and stockings, he travelled widely in Europe. Travel was one of his great interests throughout his life. He was also actively interested in politics. He wrote articles and poems attacking people's prejudices, and so angered Queen Anne that he was sent to prison from 1702-4. He was rescued from prison by a Conservative politician, who employed him as a secret agent, sending him round the country to gather information about people's political opinions. He was again sent to prison when he wrote articles criticizing King George I, but when he was set free he continued his writing.

During his life Defoe wrote over five hundred articles and books, but he is best known for the works he produced in his later years, and especially for *Robinson Crusoe*, one of the most familiar stories in English literature. This is considered by many to be the first English novel, and is based on the true story of Alexander Selkirk, a Scottish sailor. When it was published it was an immediate success. It was translated into many languages, and influenced many later writers and thinkers.

Defoe's influence on the development of the English novel was enormous. He wrote plainly and clearly, with realistic descriptions of people, places and action. His writing shows a reporter's love of detail as well as a writer's powerful imagination.

Well-known works by Daniel Defoe include: *Robinson Crusoe* (1719), *Captain Singleton* (1720), *Moll Flanders* (1722), *A Journal of the Plague Year* (1722), *Roxana* (1724), *A Tour Through the Whole Island of Great Britain* (1724-7).

Robinson Crusoe

Robinson Crusoe has had a fortunate escape from drowning. The ship he was travelling in was wrecked by a terrible storm in the Caribbean Sea, and he only just managed to reach land. However, quickly realizing that he would need provisions, he swam back to the ship before it sank completely, made a raft and brought some useful things back with him – clothes, food, guns and tools.

Now Crusoe is apparently alone in this strange country, where it seems he will have to work hard in order to survive.

My next work was to view the country and seek a proper place for my habitation, and where to stow my goods to secure them from whatever might happen. Where I was, I yet knew not; whether on the continent, or on an island; whether inhabited or not inhabited; whether in danger of wild beasts, or not. There was a hill, not above a
5   mile from me, which rose up very steep and high, and which seemed to overtop some other hills, which lay as in a ridge from it, northward. I took out one of the fowling-pieces and one of the pistols, and a horn of powder; and thus armed, I travelled for discovery up to the top of that hill, where, after I had with great labour and difficulty got to the top, I saw my fate to my great affliction, viz., that I was in an island environed
10   every way with the sea, no land to be seen, except some rocks which lay a great way off, and two small islands less than this, which lay about three leagues to the west.

    I found also that the island I was in was barren, and, as I saw good reason to believe, uninhabited, except by wild beasts, of whom, however, I saw none; yet I saw an abundance of fowls, but knew not their kinds; neither, when I killed them, could I
15   tell what was fit for food, and what not. At my coming back, I shot at a great bird which I saw sitting upon a tree on the side of a great wood. I believe it was the first gun that had been fired there since the creation of the world. I had no sooner fired, but from all the parts of the wood there arose an innumerable number of fowls of many sorts, making a confused screaming, and crying everyone according to his usual note; but not
20   one of them of any kind that I knew.

. . . . .

    Contented with this discovery, I came back to my raft, and fell to work to bring my cargo on shore, which took me up the rest of that day; and what to do with myself at night I knew not, nor indeed where to rest; for I was afraid to lie down on the ground, not knowing but some wild beast might devour me, though, as I afterwards found, there
25   was really no need for those fears. However, as well as I could I barricaded myself round with the chests and boards that I had brought on shore, and made a kind of a hut for that night's lodging.

Notes		
seek: look for	*raft:* a simple boat made of flat pieces of wood
stow: put away	*cargo:* goods carried on a boat
horn of powder: container of gunpowder	*devour me:* eat me up
viz: (*videlicet,* Latin) namely	*barricaded:* made a wall or fence
barren: with very few plants	*hut:* small shelter made of wood
fowls: birds	

Comprehension

The author

Only one ending in each group is correct. Choose the correct one.

1 Daniel Defoe travelled abroad
  a as a spy.
  b selling things.
  c to do research for his novels.
  d to avoid being sent to prison.

2 He wrote
  a romantic poetry.
  b Conservative speeches.
  c hundreds of articles.
  d his autobiography.

3 He is most famous for
  a his political views.
  b *Robinson Crusoe*.
  c his support for Queen Anne.
  d his diaries.

The text

A The words and expressions on the left are no longer in common use. Match them with their more up-to-date meanings on the right.

1	habitation	a	surrounded
2	to overtop	b	a gun for hunting birds
3	fowling-piece	c	to be higher than
4	affliction	d	a long way off, far away
5	environed	e	distress, despair
6	a great way off	f	about five kilometres
7	league	g	a place to live

B Rewrite these phrases or sentences in modern English.

1 My next work was to (line 1)
2 I yet knew not (line 3)

3 not above a mile (line 4)
4 I travelled for discovery (line 7)
5 but knew not their kinds (line 14)
6 At my coming back (line 15)
7 crying everyone according to his usual note (line 19)

C Answer these questions.

1 Why does Crusoe want to find a place to put his goods?
2 Why does he climb up the hill?
3 Why does he take a gun with him?
4 How does he feel when he knows he is on an island?
5 Why do you think he doesn't recognize the types of bird on the island?
6 Why does he think 'it was the first gun that had been fired there since the creation of the world' (line 16)? What does he mean when he says this?
7 Why is he 'contented with this discovery' (line 21)?
8 Why doesn't he want to lie down to sleep at night?
9 Why do you think 'there was really no need for those fears' (line 25)?
10 How does he manage to make himself a shelter for the night?

Discussion

1 Crusoe has brought clothes, food, guns and tools with him from the ship. Decide what items in each of these categories would be most useful on a desert island. For example, clothes: pullover? coat? shorts? an extra pair of shoes? Make a list of what you would put on your small raft, if, like Crusoe, you only had a few minutes to think about it.

2 How do you think the story is going to continue? Are there any clues in the text?

Role-play

Imagine that you and a friend are on an expedition exploring a remote part of the African jungle, and have got separated from your group. Plan what you will do about

  a the possible dangers
  b finding food and water
  c protecting yourselves
  d finding the other members of the group.

Student A: You are the adventurous type who enjoys action but who often gets into dangerous situations.

Student B: You are more cautious: your motto is 'Better safe than sorry!'

Extension

Grammar

A 'Where I was, I yet knew not' (line 2). Nowadays we would say 'I did not (yet) know where I was.' Make indirect questions from the following direct questions, starting *He asked ...*

1 'When do the banks close?'
2 'Where do they come from?'
3 'Do you speak Italian?'
4 'Did you go there yesterday?'
5 'How long have you been working here?'
6 'Have you been here before?'
7 'How long will they be staying?'
8 'Can you come here tomorrow?'
9 'Are you ready yet?'
10 'Who are you?'

B 'Whether on the continent, or on an island' (line 3). Decide whether articles are needed in the following sentences, and add *a, an,* or *the* where necessary.

1 What did you think of .... book you borrowed from me?

2 .... time is .... money.
3 London is situated in .... south-east, on .... River Thames.
4 They decided to buy .... house on .... Greek island when they retired.
5 She isn't very keen on eating .... red meat these days.
6 Robin Hood stole from .... rich and gave to .... poor.
7 I think they live near .... Lake Geneva, don't they?
8 He's .... engineer, and she's .... architect. Their children are .... artists.
9 She's played .... piano all her life.
10 I met .... friend of yours at .... party .... other day. .... party was at .... Hilton Hotel!

Negative adjectives

Uninhabited (line 13) is the negative of *inhabited.* Make the negative form of these adjectives, by adding the correct prefix.

1 intelligent
2 legible
3 practical
4 literate
5 patient
6 polite
7 fit
8 responsible
9 comfortable
10 mature
11 rational
12 convenient
13 logical
14 possible
15 fair
16 secure

Composition (120 – 180 words)

1 Continue Robinson Crusoe's story by writing a composition beginning *When I woke up the next morning, I saw to my horror that .....*

2 Which three objects would you most like to take with you to a desert island? Describe them, and explain why you have chosen them.

2

JONATHAN SWIFT

1667 – 1745

Jonathan Swift, the son of English parents, was born and educated in Dublin, Ireland. He became a secretary to an English diplomat, Sir William Temple, and through his employer he met many important political figures. When Sir William died, Swift tried hard to make a living in England, but without influence or wealth it was almost impossible for a young man to gain a good position.

In 1713, Swift became Dean of St Patrick's Cathedral in Dublin, and settled permanently in Ireland. Although he would have preferred to live in England, he worked hard for the Protestant Church in Ireland and for the Irish people: he enthusiastically supported the campaign for greater freedom for the Irish. He gave a third of his income to charities, and founded a hospital for the poor. He was greatly loved and admired in Dublin.

Perhaps influenced by the disappointments he suffered in his life, Swift became one of the greatest satirical writers in English, producing numerous poems, essays and pamphlets. In his writing he attacked all levels of society, religion and politics, with penetrating intelligence, sharp observation and wit. His most famous book is *Gulliver's Travels:* the first two parts are often popular with young readers, as light, imaginative traveller's tales, but in the last two parts the satire becomes quite savage, and this in fact caused an outcry when the book was published.

Well-known works by Jonathan Swift include: *A Tale of a Tub* (1704), *Gulliver's Travels* (1726).

Gulliver's Travels

In *A Voyage to Lilliput*, the first part of the book, Gulliver, an English ship's doctor, is shipwrecked in a storm somewhere in the Indian Ocean. He assumes his shipmates have all drowned, as he alone manages to swim to land. In this extract, he is exhausted after his long swim. He does not know what country he is in, and there is no sign of any of the inhabitants.

I lay down on the grass, which was very short and soft, where I slept sounder than ever I remember to have done in my life, and as I reckoned, above nine hours; for when I awaked, it was just daylight. I attempted to rise, but was not able to stir. For as I happened to lie on my back, I found my arms and legs were strongly fastened on each

5 side to the ground; and my hair, which was long and thick, tied down in the same manner. I likewise felt several slender ligatures across my body, from my armpits to my thighs. I could only look upwards; the sun began to grow hot, and the light offended my eyes. I heard a confused noise about me, but in the posture I lay, could see nothing except the sky.

10 In a little time I felt something alive moving on my left leg, which advancing gently forward over my breast, came almost up to my chin; when bending my eyes downwards as much as I could, I perceived it to be a human creature not six inches high, with a bow and arrow in his hands, and a quiver at his back. In the meantime, I felt at least forty more of the same kind (as I conjectured) following the first. I was in the utmost

15 astonishment, and roared so loud that they all ran back in a fright; and some of them, as I was afterwards told, were hurt with the falls they got by leaping from my sides upon the ground. However, they soon returned; and one of them, who ventured so far as to get a full sight of my face, lifting up his hands and eyes by way of admiration, cryed out in a shrill, but distinct voice, *hekinah degul.* The others repeated the same words several

20 times, but I then knew not what they meant. I lay all this while, as the reader may believe, in great uneasiness.

At length, struggling to get loose, I had the fortune to break the strings and wrench out the pegs that fastened my left arm to the ground; for, by lifting it up to my face, I discovered the methods they had taken to bind me; and, at the same time, with a violent

25 pull, which gave me excessive pain, I a little loosened the strings that tied down my hair on the left side, so that I was just able to turn my head about two inches. But the creatures ran off a second time, before I could seize them; whereupon there was a great shout in a very shrill accent. And after it ceased, I heard one of them cry aloud, *tolgo phonac;* when in an instant I felt above an hundred arrows discharged on my left hand,

30 which pricked me like so many needles. And besides, they shot another flight into the air, as we do bombs in Europe; whereof many, I suppose, fell on my body, (though I felt them not) and some on my face, which I immediately covered with my left hand.

Notes	
sounder: more soundly, more deeply	*cryed:* old-fashioned spelling of *cried*
awaked: (archaic) awoke, woke up	*shrill:* high and sharp
ligatures: ropes tying him down	*wrench out:* pull out by force
posture: position	*hekinah degul, tolgo phonac:* words in the Lilliputian
breast: chest	language
perceived it to be: realized it was	*two inches:* five centimetres
six inches: fifteen centimetres	*whereupon:* at which point
quiver: a container for arrows	*an hundred:* (archaic) a hundred
conjectured: guessed	*discharged:* shot
utmost: greatest	*whereof:* (archaic) of which
ventured: dared	

Comprehension

The author

Correct these sentences if necessary. Tick the sentences which are already correct.

1 Swift was an Irish diplomat's secretary.
2 He failed to find the job he wanted.
3 He became a politician.
4 He was a Roman Catholic.
5 He founded a school for poor children.
6 He wrote his most famous book when he was nearly sixty.
7 His life was full of successes.
8 He became the greatest satirical writer in English.

The text

A Match these words from the text with their meanings.

1	attempted (line 3)	a	tied
2	fastened (line 4)	b	worry, anxiety
3	slender (line 6)	c	good luck
4	roared (line 15)	d	thin
5	leaping (line 16)	e	get hold of, grab
6	uneasiness (line 21)	f	tried
7	fortune (line 22)	g	shouted
8	seize (line 27)	h	jumping

B Rewrite these phrases or sentences in your own words.

1 as I reckoned (line 2)
2 above nine hours (line 2)
3 was not able to stir (line 3)
4 the light offended my eyes (line 7)
5 In the meantime (line 13)
6 I was in the utmost astonishment (line 14)
7 struggling to get loose (line 22)
8 I discovered the methods they had taken to bind me (line 24)

9 which gave me excessive pain (line 25)
10 after it ceased (line 28)

C Answer these questions.

1 Why do you think Gulliver sleeps so well?
2 Why isn't he able to move when he wakes up?
3 Describe the 'human creature' (line 12) who climbs up to Gulliver's chin.
4 What happens when Gulliver shouts at the Lilliputians?
5 Suggest possible meanings for *hekinah degul* and *tolgo phonac* (lines 19 and 28).
6 How does Gulliver manage to free himself a little?
7 How do the Lilliputians react to this?
8 How does Gulliver protect himself from being injured by the arrows?

Discussion

1 How does the author show us that the people of Lilliput are really very small?

2 What do you think will happen next to Gulliver? Will he be attacked again by the little men, will they become friendly with him, or will he escape?

3 Can you imagine what Gulliver's day-to-day problems will be, if he has to stay in Lilliput for some time? How do you think the Lilliputians will look after him and provide him with food?

Role-play

Student A: You and your friend (Student B) are planning your summer holiday for next year. You only want to visit countries where you can speak the language, because you think that is the best way of getting to know the people and the customs. However, you only speak two foreign languages, so your choice of holiday destination is rather limited.

Student B: You are keen to visit several different countries. You think that being able to speak the language is useful, but not necessary. Explain to your friend how you would manage to communicate in a foreign country, even if you didn't know a word of the language.

Extension

Word-building

'In the utmost astonishment' (line 14), 'by way of admiration' (line 18). These are some of the most common noun endings: *-ment, -ation, -ity, -ence, -ance, -ness*. Turn these verbs and adjectives into nouns, making any necessary spelling changes.

1 embarrass	7 able	13 intelligent
2 dark	8 move	14 perform
3 lonely	9 sincere	15 appear
4 explain	10 argue	16 interfere
5 educate	11 secure	17 popular
6 promote	12 lazy	18 enter

Vocabulary and idioms

Check that you know all the parts of the body given below. Then complete the sentences with the correct word in the correct form. You may need to use some of the words more than once.

finger, thumb, hand, wrist, elbow, arm, armpit
toe, ankle, foot, shin, knee, thigh, leg, hip
tongue, chin, neck, shoulder, chest, breast, heart

1 Don't believe him – he must be pulling your
   .... !
2 I can't quite remember his name, but it's on the
   tip of my ....
3 He's so tactless. He's always putting his
   .... in it.
4 I can always offer you a(n) .... to cry on,
   if you want to tell me your problems.
5 He's decided to make a clean .... of it,
   and tell the police the whole truth.
6 That boy is a real pain in the .... He
   always causes trouble.

7 She can twist her father round her little
   ....
8 Children have to learn to be independent and
   stand on their own two ....
9 I'd give my right .... to be able to visit
   the Grand Canyon.
10 It broke my .... to sell my father's
   painting, but I needed the money.

Grammar

'(I) roared so loud(ly) that they all ran back ...'
(line 15). Connect the following sentences with
so/such ... that in the same way.

1 It was a beautiful day. We decided to have a picnic
   in the park.
2 There's a lot of furniture in their lounge. It's
   difficult to move around.
3 He did very little work. He failed his exams.
4 It was terrible news. We all felt quite depressed.
5 They had a wonderful holiday. They decided to
   go back to the Algarve next year.
6 There were very few spectators. The match was
   postponed.
7 Mark's boss was impressed with his work. He gave
   Mark a pay rise.
8 The recipe was very complicated. Liz couldn't
   follow it.

Composition (120 – 180 words)

1 Tell the story of Gulliver's arrival in Lilliput from
   the point of view of one of the Lilliputians. You
   might start: *I was walking along the path down to*
   the beach when suddenly I saw, lying on the grass ...

2 You have been asked to recommend a book for
   your school library to buy. Write a report on the
   text you have read, commenting on the author's
   style and the type of language used. Say whether
   you think the book this text comes from would be
   suitable for the library or not.

3

JANE AUSTEN

1775 – 1817

Jane Austen was born in Steventon in Hampshire, England. She was the daughter of a clergyman, who taught her, and encouraged her to read widely and to write. She led an uneventful domestic life and did not marry. She had five brothers and a sister, and often visited their homes or cities like London or Bath. Three of her books (*Mansfield Park, Emma, Persuasion*) were written in the busy family sitting-room.

Jane Austen is universally considered one of the greatest English novelists. As she said about writing novels, 'Three or four families in a country village is the very thing to work on.' She wrote, with penetrating observation, about English life and the social customs of the middle classes. She is famous for the intelligence and delicate irony of her writing, for the realistic characters she creates, and for the small but completely satisfying world which she describes to her readers.

Of Jane Austen's six great novels, four were published anonymously during her lifetime and the other two after her death: *Sense and Sensibility* (1811), *Pride and Prejudice* (1813), *Mansfield Park* (1814), *Emma* (1816), *Northanger Abbey* (1818) and *Persuasion* (1818).

Pride and Prejudice

A rich young gentleman has moved into the country, and is renting a large house, Netherfield Park. His name is Mr Bingley. All the mothers in the neighbourhood would like to give him the opportunity to meet their daughters as soon as possible. Mr and Mrs Bennet, who live near Netherfield Park, have *five* daughters who are all about the right age for marriage. So Mrs Bennet is especially interested in Mr Bingley.

'My dear Mr Bennet,' said his lady to him one day, 'have you heard that Netherfield Park is let at last?'

Mr Bennet replied that he had not.

'But it is,' returned she; 'for Mrs Long has just been here, and she told me all about it.'

Mr Bennet made no answer.

'Do not you want to know who has taken it?' cried his wife impatiently.

'*You* want to tell me, and I have no objection to hearing it.'

This was invitation enough.

'Why, my dear, you must know, Mrs Long says that Netherfield is taken by a young man of large fortune from the north of England; that he came down on Monday in a chaise and four to see the place, and was so much delighted with it that he agreed with Mr Morris immediately; that he is to take possession before Michaelmas, and some of his servants are to be in the house by the end of next week.'

'What is his name?'

'Bingley.'

'Is he married or single?'

'Oh! Single, my dear, to be sure! A single man of large fortune; four or five thousand a year. What a fine thing for our girls!'

'How so? How can it affect them?'

'My dear Mr Bennet,' replied his wife, 'how can you be so tiresome! You must know that I am thinking of his marrying one of them.'

'Is that his design in settling here?'

'Design! Nonsense, how can you talk so! But it is very likely that he *may* fall in love with one of them, and therefore you must visit him as soon as he comes.'

'I see no occasion for that. You and the girls may go, or you may send them by themselves, which perhaps will be still better, for as you are as handsome as any of them, Mr Bingley might like you the best of the party.'

'My dear, you flatter me. I certainly *have* had my share of beauty, but I do not pretend to be any thing extraordinary now. When a woman has five grown up daughters, she ought to give over thinking of her own beauty.'

'In such cases, a woman has not often much beauty to think of.'

'But, my dear, you must indeed go and see Mr Bingley when he comes into the neighbourhood.'

'It is more than I engage for, I assure you.'

'But consider your daughters. Only think what an establishment it would be for one of them. Sir William and Lady Lucas are determined to go, merely on that account, for in general you know they visit no new comers. Indeed you must go, for it will be impossible for *us* to visit him, if you do not.'

'You are over scrupulous surely. I dare say Mr Bingley will be very glad to see you; and I will send a few lines by you to assure him of my hearty consent to his marrying which ever he chuses of the girls; though I must throw in a good word for my little Lizzy.'

Notes	*My dear Mr Bennet:* it was usual in the early nineteenth century for husbands and wives to speak to each other formally like this	large income at the time

Notes *My dear Mr Bennet:* it was usual in the early nineteenth century for husbands and wives to speak to each other formally like this
let: rented
cried: said loudly
of large fortune: wealthy
chaise and four: carriage with four horses
Michaelmas: end of September
four or five thousand: £4000 or £5000 a year, a very large income at the time
party: group
flatter: pay compliments to, praise exaggeratedly
any thing: usually written as one word these days
engage for: promise to do
establishment: (here) marriage
over scrupulous: too worried about being polite
chuses: old spelling of *chooses*
Lizzy: short for Elizabeth

Comprehension

Decide whether these sentences are true (**T**) or false (**F**).

1 Jane Austen married a clergyman.
2 She had five brothers and a sister.
3 She was taught by her father.
4 She often travelled abroad.
5 Her novels are usually set in a fashionable town.

The text

A Find words or expressions in the text which mean approximately the same as these words or phrases.

1 his wife
2 replied
3 annoying
4 plan, intention
5 probable
6 reason
7 attractive
8 adult
9 stop, give up
10 sincere, enthusiastic

B Rewrite these phrases or sentences in your own words.

1 I have no objection to hearing it (line 7)
2 This was invitation enough (line 8)
3 he agreed with Mr Morris (line 11)
4 he is to take possession (line 12)
5 How so? (line 19)
6 I see no occasion for that (line 25)
7 I do not pretend to be any thing extraordinary now (line 28)
8 when he comes into the neighbourhood (line 32)
9 merely on that account (line 36)
10 throw in a good word (line 41)

C Answer these questions.

1 Identify these characters in the text:
   a the owner of Netherfield Park
   b a neighbour
   c one of the Bennets' daughters
   d neighbours with an unmarried daughter.
2 Why is Mrs Bennet so excited by Mr Bingley's arrival?
3 'How can it affect them?' (line 19). Does Mr Bennet really not understand his wife, or is he just pretending? If so, why?
4 'Mr Bingley might like you the best of the party' (line 27). Is Mr Bennet serious in saying this? Does Mrs Bennet take him seriously?
5 'I will send a few lines by you ...' (line 40). Is Mr Bennet really going to send Mr Bingley a letter? Why does he say this?
6 What can we learn of Mr and Mrs Bennet's characters, and their relationship, from this text?

Discussion

1 This extract comes from the beginning of the book. What do you think is going to happen in the rest of the book?
2 Can you imagine why Jane Austen called this book *Pride and Prejudice*?
3 In many countries parents still arrange marriages for their children. What are the advantages and possible disadvantages of this system?

Role-play

Student A: You are a teenager who is hoping to go to a special late-night party/concert/performance. You want to go very much, because all your friends are going, and you have already bought the ticket and arranged transport. You now have to persuade your father and mother (Students B and C) to agree to let you go.

Student B: You are the mother. Although you want your son/daughter to enjoy him/herself, you are worried about him/her coming home late. Ask how and when he/she plans to come home.

Student C: You are the father. You think young people today expect too much. When you were young, you seldom had the money or opportunity to go out as often as your son/daughter does. You are also rather disappointed with his/her schoolwork, and think he/she should stay at home to study.

Extension

Grammar

A 'You must visit him as soon as he comes' (line 24). Complete the following sentences with the correct form of these verbs: *be call dismiss get back leave receive save up send start.*

1 I've got to go now. I'll see you when I ....

2 You must wait here until the doctor .... your name.

3 We'd like to visit Acapulco after we .... to Mexico City.

4 You must finish the report before the meeting ....

5 I won't be able to apply for the job until they .... me the details.

6 You will come to see me before you ...., won't you?

7 I'll fax you the information as soon as I .... it.

8 Before you .... him, you'd better find a replacement.

9 When he .... enough money, he's going to buy a flat.

B 'He agreed with Mr Morris immediately' (line 11). Complete the following sentences with the correct adverb from this list: *unfortunately nearly well seldom suddenly comfortably soon monotonously easily.* There is one word more than you need.

1 He read the speech so .... that some of the audience fell asleep.

2 I .... missed the bus. I had to run for it.

3 She .... smiles at anyone. She's very bad-tempered.

4 That's very good work. You did that very ....

5 The old man settled back .... into his favourite armchair.

6 You'll be moving to Berlin ...., won't you?

7 .... there was a loud crash from the next room.

8 .... the company didn't offer me the job I wanted.

Composition (120 – 180 words)

1 Should a husband and wife be the same age or the same nationality? Should they come from a similar background, be of the same class or religion, share the same interests? Write down your ideas.

2 How important is money in marriage? Would financial considerations affect your decision to marry? Explain your views.

4

EMILY BRONTË

1818 – 1848

Emily Brontë was born in Thornton in Yorkshire, England, the fifth of six children. In 1820 the family moved to Haworth (also in Yorkshire) when their father became rector of the village church. Apart from a short unhappy period at boarding school, Emily was educated mostly at home. She was especially close to her younger sister Anne. As she was growing up, she wrote some fine dramatic poetry, and created her own imaginary world. She was more attached than any of her sisters to the wild moorland scenery round Haworth. She worked as a governess for a short time, and even went to Brussels to study languages with her sister Charlotte, but she could not stay away from her beloved moors for long.

Not very much is known about Emily's personal life: she had no close friends and wrote few letters. Living conditions in the small village on the bleak Yorkshire moors at the time of the Industrial Revolution were extremely bad, and it is extraordinary that Emily and her sisters managed to make such an important contribution to English literature. They had a constant struggle with illness and family problems. Emily's early death was due to tuberculosis, a disease of the lungs which was fairly common in the last century.

Emily Brontë's poetry is currently admired by critics, for its originality and deep feeling, but she will always be remembered for her great and only novel *Wuthering Heights* (1847), a work of dark, brooding violence and passion. 1847 is an important landmark in the history of the English novel: all three Brontë sisters published major novels in that year (Charlotte Brontë: *Jane Eyre*, Anne Brontë: *Agnes Grey*).

Wuthering Heights

Heathcliff is an orphan boy who is taken to live with the Earnshaw family at Wuthering Heights, in a remote, wild part of Yorkshire. He and Catherine Earnshaw grow to love each other passionately, but Catherine decides to marry her handsome but weak neighbour, Edgar Linton. When she dies in childbirth, leaving a daughter, who is also called Catherine, Heathcliff plans his revenge on both the Earnshaw and Linton families.

In this extract, Heathcliff intends to force young Catherine to marry his sickly son Linton. He persuades the girl to come to his house, Wuthering Heights, with her nurse, Nelly Dean, and plans to keep her there until the marriage ceremony can be performed.

We reached the threshold; Catherine walked in; and I stood waiting till she had conducted the invalid to a chair, expecting her out immediately, when Mr. Heathcliff, pushing me forward, exclaimed –

'My house is not stricken with the plague, Nelly; and I have a mind to be hospitable today. Sit down, and allow me to shut the door.'

He shut and locked it also. I started.

'You shall have tea, before you go home,' he added. 'I am by myself. Hareton is gone with some cattle to the Lees – and Zillah and Joseph are off on a journey of pleasure. And, though I'm used to being alone, I'd rather have some interesting company, if I can get it. Miss Linton, take your seat by *him*. I give you what I have; the present is hardly worth accepting; but, I have nothing else to offer. It is Linton, I mean. How she does stare! It's odd what a savage feeling I have to anything that seems afraid of me!'

• • • • •

He drew in his breath, struck the table, and swore to himself.

'By hell! I hate them.'

'I'm not afraid of you!' exclaimed Catherine. • • •

She stepped close up, her black eyes flashing with passion and resolution.

'Give me that key – I will have it!' she said. 'I wouldn't eat or drink here, if I were starving.'

Heathcliff had the key in his hand that remained on the table. He looked up, seized with a sort of surprise at her boldness, or, possibly, reminded by her voice and glance of the person from whom she inherited it.

She snatched at the instrument, and half succeeded in getting it out of his loosened fingers; but her action recalled him to the present; he recovered it speedily.

'Now, Catherine Linton,' he said, 'stand off, or I shall knock you down; and that will make Mrs. Dean mad.'

Regardless of this warning, she captured his closed hand and its contents again.

'We *will* go!' she repeated, exerting her utmost efforts to cause the iron muscles to relax; and finding that her nails made no impression, she applied her teeth pretty sharply.

Heathcliff glanced at me a glance that kept me from interfering a moment. Catherine was too intent on his fingers to notice his face. He opened them, suddenly, and resigned the object of dispute; but, ere she had well secured it, he seized her with the liberated hand, and, pulling her on his knee, administered with the other a shower of terrific slaps on both sides of the head, each sufficient to have fulfilled his threat, had she been able to fall.

At this diabolical violence, I rushed on him furiously.

'You villain!' I began to cry, 'you villain!'

A touch on the chest silenced me; I am stout, and soon put out of breath; and, what with that and the rage, I staggered dizzily back, and felt ready to suffocate, or to burst a blood vessel.

The scene was over in two minutes; Catherine, released, put her two hands to her temples, and looked just as if she were not sure whether her ears were off or on.

Notes	*threshold:* doorway	*liberated:* freed
	invalid: a sick person	*slaps:* blows with the palm of the hand
	hospitable: welcoming	*diabolical:* devilish, evil
	Hareton, Zillah and Joseph: people who work for Heathcliff	*stout:* overweight
	started: jumped with surprise	*rage:* anger
	cattle: cows	*staggered:* moved unsteadily, almost falling over
	ere: (poetic) before	*suffocate:* be unable to breathe
		temples: sides of the forehead

Comprehension

The author

Correct these sentences if necessary. Tick the sentences which are already correct.

1 Emily Brontë was born in Yorkshire.
2 She was the youngest of a large family.
3 She often went abroad.
4 She wrote several important novels.
5 She was closest to her sister Charlotte.
6 She wrote few letters in her long life.
7 She spent most of her childhood at boarding school.
8 She died of an illness.

The text

A Rewrite these phrases or sentences in your own words.

1 stricken with the plague (line 4)
2 I have a mind to (line 4)
3 I will have it (line 17)
4 the instrument (line 22)
5 he recovered it speedily (line 23)
6 stand off (line 24)
7 Regardless of this warning (line 26)
8 exerting her utmost efforts (line 27)
9 she applied her teeth (line 28)
10 (he) resigned the object of dispute (line 30)
11 ere she had well secured it (line 31)
12 had she been able to fall (line 33)

B Match these words from the text with their meanings.

1	conducted (line 2)	a	determination
2	savage (line 12)	b	used bad language
3	struck (line 13)	c	hit
4	swore (line 13)	d	wicked man
5	exclaimed (line 15)	e	angrily
6	resolution (line 16)	f	wild, violent
7	furiously (line 35)	g	led
8	villain (line 36)	h	shouted

C Answer these questions.

1 How do you know that Nelly Dean expects Catherine to leave the house almost immediately?
2 Who do you think 'the invalid' is?
3 Why does Heathcliff lock the door?
4 What does Heathcliff mean by saying Linton is a 'present' (line 10)?
5 How does the author show how violent Heathcliff can be? Find examples.
6 'By hell! I hate them' (line 14). Who do you think Heathcliff means by 'them'?
7 Who is the person Catherine has inherited her boldness from? Why does her spirited answer make Heathcliff pause for a moment?
8 'Sufficient to have fulfilled his threat' (line 33). What was Heathcliff's threat?
9 Why do you think Nelly does not interfere until Heathcliff slaps Catherine?
10 Why is Catherine so shocked when Heathcliff hits her?

Discussion

1 Do you think Heathcliff will succeed in forcing Catherine to marry Linton? What do you think will happen in the end? Will Heathcliff get his revenge or not? What kind of revenge do you think he is planning?

2 What do you know about the characters of Heathcliff, Catherine and Nelly Dean? Describe them as far as possible.

3 How would you react to being locked in Heathcliff's house, if you were Catherine?

Extension

Vocabulary

'I rushed on him furiously' (line 35). These adjectives are graded, from 'slightly angry' to 'extremely angry': *cross, annoyed, angry, furious*. Now you grade the following groups of words in the same way.

1 small   big   huge   tiny   gigantic
2 interesting   dull   fascinating   routine
3 freezing   boiling   warm   hot   tepid   cool   cold
4 disgusting   tasty   delicious   nice   tasteless
5 overjoyed   satisfied   happy   delighted   miserable   unhappy
6 good   evil   angelic   naughty   bad   wicked

Grammar

'Succeeded *in* getting it' (line 22). Complete the sentences with the gerund form of the verb in brackets, and one of these prepositions: *in, of, on, to.*

1 I'll never get used .... (get up) so early.
2 She's looking forward .... (see) her friends soon.
3 The customer insisted .... (have) a refund.

4 Do you object .... (do) the washing-up?
5 We're very fond .... (listen) to jazz.
6 Are you interested .... (apply for) that job?
7 I've always been terrified .... (fly).

Expressions

'I am by myself' (line 7). Use an expression with *by* to complete the second sentence so that it means the same as the first.

1 I've missed the post. I'll have to deliver this letter myself.
   I've missed the post. I'll have to deliver this letter ....

2 Can I use my credit card to pay the bill?
   Can I pay ....?

3 I haven't been introduced to Mr Biggs, but I'd recognize him.
   I haven't been introduced to Mr Biggs, but I know ....

4 I'm afraid I accidentally put the wrong letter in the envelope.
   I'm afraid I ....

5 I didn't plan to meet him.
   I met him ....

6 I'm taking the car to the conference.
   I'm going to the conference ....

7 You'll have to give the speech without referring to any notes.
   You'll have to learn ....

Composition (120 – 180 words)

1 Write a story beginning *He pushed me into the room. The door banged behind me, and I heard the key turn in the lock.*

2 What does the physical violence in this text tell us about Heathcliff and Catherine, their characters and their relationship? Write down your opinions.

5

CHARLOTTE BRONTË

1816 – 1855

Charlotte Brontë was born in Thornton in Yorkshire, England, the daughter of a clergyman. Her mother died in 1821, so four of the Brontë daughters were sent to a boarding school (which Charlotte portrayed as Lowood school in *Jane Eyre*). Charlotte blamed this school for the early deaths of her two older sisters Maria and Elizabeth, and for her own poor health in later life. At home the girls and their brother Branwell read widely, and invented and wrote highly imaginative stories.

Charlotte taught as a governess in two private families, and then, in her early twenties, went to Brussels to study languages. She fell deeply in love with her French teacher, and suffered greatly when he did not reply to the letters she wrote to him after returning home.

Charlotte helped her sisters Emily and Anne to publish their first novels, and began to write *Jane Eyre*. Although this novel was very successful, Charlotte was now living through a tragic period in her personal life. Branwell and Emily died in the same year, 1848, and her remaining sister Anne the following spring. In spite of this great emotional loss, and the terrible loneliness which followed, she struggled to continue writing. In 1854, after some hesitation, she agreed to marry her father's assistant, Arthur Nicholls, but she died a few months after her wedding, when she was expecting their first child.

Charlotte Brontë is widely praised for her depth of feeling and the realism of her writing. Her works continue to be read and appreciated. Her most famous novel is *Jane Eyre* (1847), which has great emotional interest and narrative power. Her other published works are: *Shirley* (1849), *Villette* (1853) and *The Professor*, her first novel, published in 1857 after her death.

Jane Eyre

Jane Eyre's parents are dead, and she has no money, so she is working as a governess at Thornfield Hall, teaching the illegitimate daughter of Mr Rochester. He is a strange man, moody and sometimes rude, but Jane is attracted to him despite his faults. There is also something strange about Thornfield Hall. Jane has heard curious wild laughter coming from an upstairs room, and seen a servant, Grace Poole, who lives and works in the attic, quite separately from the other servants.

I started wide awake on hearing a vague murmur, peculiar and lugubrious, which sounded, I thought, just above me. I wished I had kept my candle burning: the night was drearily dark; my spirits were depressed. I rose and sat up in bed, listening. The sound was hushed.

5   I tried again to sleep; but my heart beat anxiously: my inward tranquillity was broken. The clock, far down in the hall, struck two. Just then it seemed my chamber door was touched, as if fingers had swept the panels in groping a way along the dark gallery outside. I said, 'Who is there?' Nothing answered. I was chilled with fear.

All at once I remembered that it might be Pilot, who, when the kitchen door chanced
10   to be left open, not infrequently found his way up to the threshold of Mr Rochester's chamber: I had seen him lying there myself in the mornings. The idea calmed me somewhat: I lay down. Silence composes the nerves; and as an unbroken hush now reigned again through the whole house, I began to feel the return of slumber. But it was not fated that I should sleep that night. A dream had scarcely approached my ear, when
15   it fled affrighted, scared by a marrow-freezing incident enough.

This was a demoniac laugh – low, suppressed, and deep – uttered, as it seemed, at the very keyhole of my chamber door. The head of my bed was near the door, and I thought at first the goblin-laughter stood at my bedside – or rather crouched by my pillow. But I rose, looked round, and could see nothing; while, as I still gazed, the
20   unnatural sound was reiterated: and I knew it came from behind the panels. My first impulse was to rise and fasten the bolt; my next again to cry out, 'Who is there?'

Something gurgled and moaned. Ere long, steps retreated up the gallery towards the third-storey staircase: a door had lately been made to shut in that staircase; I heard it open and close, and all was still.

25   'Was that Grace Poole? And is she possessed with a devil?' thought I. Impossible now to remain longer by myself; I must go to Mrs Fairfax. I hurried on my frock and a shawl; I withdrew the bolt and opened the door with a trembling hand. There was a candle burning just outside, and on the matting in the gallery. I was surprised at this circumstance. But still more was I amazed to perceive the air quite dim, as if filled with
30   smoke; and, while looking to the right hand and left, to find whence these blue wreaths issued, I became further aware of a strong smell of burning.

Something creaked: it was a door ajar; and that door was Mr Rochester's, and the smoke rushed in a cloud from thence. I thought no more of Mrs Fairfax; I thought no more of Grace Poole, or the laugh: in an instant, I was within the chamber. Tongues of
35   flame darted round the bed: the curtains were on fire. In the midst of blaze and vapour, Mr Rochester lay stretched motionless, in deep sleep.

Notes	*started wide awake:* woke up with a jump	*marrow-freezing:* horrifying

Notes

started wide awake: woke up with a jump	*marrow-freezing:* horrifying
lugubrious: mournful	*demoniac:* devilish
drearily: depressingly	*goblin:* a small devil
hushed: silenced	*crouched:* bent down
chamber: a bedroom	*reiterated:* repeated
panels: wooden wall covering	*gurgled:* made a bubbling sound
groping: feeling the way	*ere:* (poetic) before
chilled: cold	*all was still:* everything was quiet
Pilot: Mr Rochester's dog	*Mrs Fairfax:* the housekeeper
not infrequently: often	*frock:* a dress
threshold: doorway	*matting:* floor covering
composes: makes calm	*whence:* (archaic) from where
fled: vanished, disappeared	*wreaths:* (here) circles of smoke
affrighted: (archaic) frightened	*thence:* (archaic) from there

Comprehension

The author

Correct these sentences if necessary. Tick the sentences which are already correct.

1 Charlotte Brontë liked her first boarding school.
2 She became a teacher in Brussels.
3 She finally married her French teacher.
4 She had four sisters and a brother.
5 She stayed in Yorkshire all her life.

The text

A Match these words or phrases from the text with their meanings.

1	murmur (line 1)	a	came out
2	tranquillity (line 5)	b	pulled back
3	hush (line 12)	c	silence
4	slumber (line 13)	d	low sound
5	withdrew (line 27)	e	slightly open
6	amazed (line 29)	f	notice
7	perceive (line 29)	g	not bright
8	dim (line 29)	h	calmness
9	issued (line 31)	i	very surprised
10	ajar (line 32)	j	sleep

B Answer these questions.

1 What makes Jane wake up?
2 What time is it?
3 Why is she frightened?
4 What is so terrifying about the 'demoniac laugh' (line 16)?
5 Why does Jane think her visitor might have been Grace Poole?
6 What two things surprise Jane when she opens the door?
7 Why does she go into Mr Rochester's room?
8 What does she find there?

C Match these nouns with the sounds they make. All the verbs are from the text.

1	a floorboard	a	moans
2	a baby	b	strikes
3	a sick person	c	beats
4	a heart	d	gurgles
5	a clock	e	murmurs
6	a voice	f	creaks

Discussion

1 What do you think Jane does next?
2 How do you think the fire started?
3 Have you ever been frightened by a strange incident or noise in the night?

Role-play

Students A and B: You are both looking for summer jobs in England next year. Consider the following advertisements, and decide which you would prefer.

> Au pair wanted for English family in London for three months. To look after two boys, aged 3 and 5. Must be able to drive. Non-smoker. £30 a week pocket-money. Some light housework.

> Group leader for foreign students spending study holidays in Britain, Edinburgh, London and Cambridge. Must be over 25, responsible, have clean driving licence and good English. No experience necessary. £150 a week. 7 days a week, 8.30 a.m. to 8 p.m.

> Seasonal workers needed for fruit factory in Sussex (S.E. England). No experience necessary. Age over 18. Must work a minimum of two months. Hours: 9 a.m. to 6 p.m. Monday to Friday. Good wages. Extra payment for night-shift.

Extension

Grammar

'I wished I had kept my candle burning' (line 2). Make sentences beginning *I wish* expressing regrets about these situations.

1 It was a mistake to buy that car – I realize that now.
2 What a pity she married him!
3 You should have told me the truth, you know.
4 It would have been better if I'd never started smoking.
5 Why on earth did you invite those awful people?
6 It was stupid of me to be so rude to him.
7 You could have given me that advice earlier.
8 I regret moving to the village now.

Vocabulary

A 'Marrow-freezing' (line 15) is an unusual compound adjective which means 'very frightening.' Match these more common compound adjectives with their meanings. Then think of a noun that each one could describe.

1 breathtaking   a terrifying
2 mouthwatering   b very sad and upsetting
3 ear-splitting   c delicious
4 life-threatening   d very dangerous
5 blood-curdling   e very loud
6 heart-rending   f exciting, wonderful

B Choose the correct word associated with fire or heat to complete each sentence.

1 Clouds of thick, black .... billowed from the factory chimney. (steam/smoke)
2 I saw the red .... of his cigarette in the darkness. (gleam/glow)
3 The building was .... out of control by the time the fire brigade arrived. (blazing/flaming)
4 You should never use petrol when trying to .... a barbecue. (fire/light)
5 If we're having a bonfire, we could bake some potatoes in the .... (ashes/sparks)

Composition (120 – 180 words)

1 Write a story beginning with these words: *I woke up with a start. I had heard a strange noise ...* or ending with these words: *Suddenly I woke up. It had all been a horrible dream!*

2 Write a formal letter of application for one of the jobs in the role-play exercise. Explain why you think you are the right person for the job.

6

WILLIAM THACKERAY

1811 – 1863

William Makepeace Thackeray was born in Calcutta, India, the only son of a British official in the East India Company. He was sent home to England to be educated. He left Cambridge without taking a degree, then trained to be a barrister, but never practised law. He began his career in journalism by becoming the owner of a weekly newspaper, which, however, had to close down a year later. Next he studied art in London and Paris, but by the end of 1833 all his inherited money had gone and he turned again to journalism to make his living. He returned to London in 1836 and contributed regularly to many magazines and newspapers. Unfortunately his wife had a mental breakdown after the birth of their third child, which broke up the family home.

Thackeray became well known as a writer in the 1840s, publishing articles, humorous sketches, stories and novels. He went on lecture tours in England and North America, and stood unsuccessfully for Parliament. He died suddenly in London at the age of 52.

Although he was a successful journalist, Thackeray's literary fame was established following publication of his best work *Vanity Fair,* widely regarded as one of the finest novels in English. It appeared in instalments, and public interest in it grew month by month. The book gives a satirical picture of a worldly society, and is still considered a witty and observant portrayal of character and the class system.

Well-known works by William Thackeray include: *Vanity Fair* (1848), *Pendennis* (1848), *Henry Esmond* (1852), *The Newcomes* (1855).

Vanity Fair

In this story we follow the lives of the two main characters, Rebecca (Becky) Sharp, the penniless daughter of an artist, and Amelia Sedley, the child of a rich London businessman. The two girls are completely different in character as well as background, but have been educated at the same school in Chiswick, Miss Pinkerton's Academy for young ladies. Rebecca, a social climber, knows that Amelia may be able to help her in life, and has managed to get herself invited to the Sedley mansion in the smartest part of London. Here she meets Amelia's older brother, Joseph, a wealthy government official who has just returned to England from his post in India.

When Rebecca saw the two magnificent cashmere shawls which Joseph Sedley had brought home to his sister, she said, with perfect truth, that 'it must be delightful to have a brother,' and easily got the pity of the tender-hearted Amelia, for being alone in the world, an orphan without friends or kindred.

5   'Not alone,' said Amelia. 'You know, Rebecca, I shall always be your friend, and love you as a sister – indeed I will.'

'Ah, but to have parents, as you have – kind, rich, affectionate parents, who give you everything you ask for; and their love, which is more precious than all! My poor papa could give me nothing, and I had but two frocks in all the world! And then to have a

10   brother, a dear brother! Oh, how you must love him!'

Amelia laughed.

'What! *Don't* you love him? You, who say you love everybody?'

'Yes, of course, I do – only –'

'Only what?'

15   'Only Joseph doesn't seem to care much whether I love him or not. He gave me two fingers to shake when he arrived after ten years' absence! He is very kind and good, but he scarcely ever speaks to me; I think he loves his pipe a great deal better than his ...' But here Amelia checked herself, for why should she speak ill of her brother? 'He was very kind to me as a child,' she added; 'I was but five years old when he went

20   away.'

'Isn't he very rich?' said Rebecca. 'They say all Indian nabobs are enormously rich.'

'I believe he has a very large income.'

'And is your sister-in-law a nice pretty woman?'

'La! Joseph is not married,' said Amelia, laughing again.

25   Perhaps she had mentioned the fact already to Rebecca, but that young lady did not appear to have remembered it; indeed, vowed and protested that she expected to see a number of Amelia's nephews and nieces. She was quite disappointed that Mr. Sedley was not married; she was sure Amelia had said he was, and she doted so on little children.

30   'I think you must have had enough of them at Chiswick,' said Amelia, rather wondering at the sudden tenderness on her friend's part; and indeed in later days Miss Sharp would never have committed herself so far as to advance opinions the untruth of which would have been so easily detected. But we must remember that she is but nineteen as yet, unused to the art of deceiving, poor innocent creature! and making her

35   own experience in her own person. The meaning of the above series of queries, as translated in the heart of this ingenious young woman, was simply this: 'If Mr Joseph Sedley is rich and unmarried, why should I not marry him! I have only a fortnight, to be sure, but there is no harm in trying.' And she determined within herself to make this laudable attempt.

Notes	
magnificent: fine, beautiful	*Indian nabob:* a European who made a fortune in India
cashmere: expensive soft wool	
shawl: a piece of cloth that a woman puts round her shoulders	*La!:* a ladylike expression of surprise
	vowed: insisted
orphan: someone whose parents are dead	*doted on:* loved very much
kindred: family	*Chiswick:* a smart area of London, where Miss Pinkerton's Academy was
frock: dress	
He gave me two fingers to shake: an emotional greeting was not considered socially correct in the early 19th century, and Joseph is a great follower of fashion	*detected:* discovered
	ingenious: clever
	laudable: praiseworthy, worth doing

Comprehension

The author

Decide whether the following sentences are true (**T**) or false (**F**).

1 William Thackeray was sent back to England with his brothers.
2 He did not practise as a lawyer.
3 He became the owner of a daily newspaper.
4 He went on to study art in London and Florence.
5 He and his wife did not have any children.
6 Nowadays he is best known for *Vanity Fair*.
7 He eventually became a Member of Parliament.
8 He lived a long and happy life.

The text

A Rewrite these phrases or sentences in your own words.

1 she said, with perfect truth (line 2)
2 the tender-hearted Amelia (line 3)
3 why should she speak ill of her brother? (line 18)
4 Miss Sharp would never have committed herself so far as to advance opinions the untruth of which would have been so easily detected (line 31)
5 she is but nineteen as yet (line 33)
6 unused to the art of deceiving (line 34)
7 she determined within herself to make this laudable attempt (line 38)

B Find expressions in the text which mean the same as these words or phrases

1 loving
2 valuable
3 being somewhere else
4 hardly
5 stopped herself
6 money received
7 your brother's wife
8 gentleness
9 questions
10 two weeks

C Complete the sentences in your own words.

1 Amelia pities her friend because Rebecca ....
2 Amelia's parents are much .... than Rebecca's were.
3 Amelia thinks that Joseph ....
4 Rebecca doesn't seem to remember ....
5 Amelia is rather surprised to hear ....
6 Rebecca decides to ....

Discussion

1 What does Rebecca want to find out about Joseph Sedley? What do you think she is most interested in: love, a career, having children or money?

2 Can you discover any of the lies which Rebecca tells? Why does she tell them, and why does Amelia believe her?

3 Will Rebecca succeed in her plan? Do you want her to?

4 'This laudable attempt' (line 38) is an example of Thackeray's irony. Find another example where

the author says the opposite of what he really means. Do you find this writing amusing? Who or what do you think Thackeray is laughing at?

Extension

Vocabulary

A Match these words connected with the family with their definitions.

1	mother-in-law	a	your brother or sister's daughter
2	niece	b	your father or mother's uncle
3	stepfather	c	your mother's husband (not your father)
4	half-brother	d	your uncle or aunt's child
5	fiancé(e)	e	your husband or wife's mother
6	cousin	f	your grandfather's or grandmother's mother
7	great-grandmother	g	the son of one of your parents
8	great-uncle	h	the man (or woman) you are engaged to marry

B 'A very large income' (line 22). These words are all connected with money: *pension salary tips pocket-money fine cash refund grant mortgage rent deposit.* Use them to complete the sentences. There are three words more than you need.

1 It isn't good for children to get too much ....

2 I can't afford to pay for the computer all at once. I'll just put down a .... and pay the rest in monthly instalments.

3 The police stopped me for speeding, and I had to pay an on-the-spot ....

4 'This cassette-recorder simply doesn't work.' 'You should ask the shop for a ....'

5 When he retired, he was worried he might not be able to manage on his ....

6 The waiters at the café aren't paid much, but they earn quite a lot in ....

7 She doesn't buy many new clothes because she's living on a student's ....

8 He turned down the new job because the .... wasn't high enough.

Grammar

'She was sure Amelia had said he was ...' (line 28). Put the following direct statements into reported speech.

1 'I'm sorry I won't be there,' he said.
2 'You've taken my keys!' she said to her husband.
3 'The Cray brothers didn't have anything to do with it,' said the policeman.
4 'Unfortunately I couldn't get there in time,' the doctor said.
5 'Tom's always been my friend,' the film star said.
6 'I think Sue's in the library,' said Edward.
7 'We must be home by 11.30,' they said.
8 'The children never drink milk with their meals,' said the woman.
9 'I don't know if I can finish the work,' the sculptor said.
10 'I hope he's looking after you,' my mother said.

Composition (120 – 180 words)

1 What impression do you get of the characters of the two girls in Thackeray's story? Think of as many adjectives as you can to describe them both, and compare their characters.

2 What are the advantages and disadvantages of being an only child (like Rebecca), or of coming from a large family?

7

CHARLES DICKENS

1812 – 1870

Charles Dickens was born in Portsea in Hampshire, England. He did not have a happy childhood. His father was a clerk who loved his family but often owed money. At the age of twelve Charles was sent to work in a factory, and had to work twelve hours a day. When his father was sent to prison for debt, the whole family had to live in the prison for a time. This unhappy experience left a strong impression on Charles. Later he worked in a lawyer's office, and then as a journalist.

Dickens' writing was published in monthly instalments in magazines, and soon became extremely popular. He produced a large number of novels and short stories, and he travelled round Britain and the United States, giving readings of his works. He was highly successful and well paid, but overwork contributed to his early death.

Dickens is one of the best-known English novelists. His books have probably been read by more people than any other English works of fiction, and they are still widely read today. He was a strong critic of the social injustice of Victorian England, publicizing issues such as child labour, poor working conditions and poverty, all of which he experienced in his childhood. He was an excellent storyteller, with a keen ear for dialogue and dialect. However, he is best known for the great variety of characters in his writing, and for the humour and sympathy with which he describes them and their lives.

Well-known works by Charles Dickens include: *The Pickwick Papers* (1837), *Oliver Twist* (1838), *Nicholas Nickleby* (1839), *The Old Curiosity Shop* (1841), *A Christmas Carol* (1843), *David Copperfield* (1850), *Bleak House* (1853), *A Tale of Two Cities* (1859), *Great Expectations* (1861).

Great Expectations

A young boy called Pip is telling the story. As his parents have both died, he is living with his older sister and her husband in a village on the Kent marshes. At the beginning of the story he helped an escaped prisoner, who will play an important part in Pip's later life. In this famous extract, he meets another person who is going to influence his life, the strange Miss Havisham.

I entered, and found myself in a pretty large room, well lighted with wax candles. No glimpse of daylight was to be seen in it. In an armchair, with an elbow resting on the table and her head leaning on that hand, sat the strangest lady I have ever seen, or shall ever see.

5 She was dressed in rich materials – satins, and lace, and silks – all of white. Her shoes were white. And she had a long white veil dependent from her hair, and she had bridal flowers in her hair, but her hair was white. Some bright jewels sparkled on her neck and on her hands, and some other jewels lay sparkling on the table. Dresses, less splendid than the dress she wore, and half-packed trunks, were scattered about. She had 10 not quite finished dressing, for she had but one shoe on – the other was on the table near her hand – her veil was but half arranged, her watch and chain were not put on, and some lace for her bosom lay with those trinkets, and with her handkerchief, and gloves, and some flowers, and a prayer-book, all confusedly heaped about the looking-glass.

15 It was not in the first moments that I saw all these things, though I saw more of them in the first moments than might be supposed. But I saw that everything within my view which ought to be white, had been white long ago, and had lost its lustre, and was faded and yellow. I saw that the bride within the bridal dress had withered like the dress, and like the flowers, and had no brightness left but the brightness of her sunken 20 eyes. I saw that the dress had been put upon the rounded figure of a young woman, and that the figure upon which it now hung loose, had shrunk to skin and bone. Once, I had been taken to see some ghastly waxwork at the fair, representing I know not what impossible personage lying in state. Once, I had been taken to one of our old marsh churches to see a skeleton in the ashes of a rich dress, that had been dug out of a vault 25 under the church pavement. Now, waxwork and skeleton seemed to have dark eyes that moved and looked at me. I would have cried out, if I could.

'Who is it?' said the lady at the table.

'Pip, ma'am.'

'Pip?'

30 'Mr Pumblechook's boy, ma'am. Come – to play.'

'Come nearer; let me look at you. Come close.'

It was when I stood before her, avoiding her eyes, that I took note of the surrounding objects in detail, and saw that her watch had stopped at twenty minutes to nine, and that a clock in the room had stopped at twenty minutes to nine.

Notes	
veil: a head-dress for a bride	*withered:* grown old and dry
dependent: (old-fashioned) hanging	*shrunk:* (from shrink) become smaller
trunks: large suitcases	*waxwork:* statue made of wax
bosom: her chest, or front of her dress	*lying in state:* on public view before being buried
trinkets: little ornaments or jewels, not worth much	*marsh:* an area of low, wet land
looking-glass: (old-fashioned) a mirror	*skeleton:* a dead person's bones
lustre: shine, brightness	*Mr Pumblechook:* Pip's uncle, who arranged this visit

Comprehension

The author

Decide whether these sentences are true (**T**) or false (**F**).

1 Charles Dickens was at school until he was fourteen.
2 He worked in a factory all his life.
3 He had several jobs before becoming a famous novelist.
4 People used to read his novels one episode at a time.
5 He worked hard as a writer to pay his debts.

The text

A Match these words from the text with their meanings.

1 glimpse (line 2)   a piled
2 heaped (line 13)   b awful, frightening
3 faded (line 18)   c an important person
4 ghastly (line 22)   d a flash, sight
5 personage (line 23) e an underground room
6 vault (line 24)   f become old and dull

B Find phrases or sentences in the text which have the same meanings as the ones below.

1 quite a big room   5 was no longer bright
2 not as beautiful as   6 I wanted to cry out, but I couldn't
3 all over the room   7 not looking directly at her
4 only had one shoe on   8 observed things around me carefully

C Answer these questions

1 How old do you imagine Miss Havisham is?
2 Why is she dressed in white?
3 Why is Pip so frightened of her?
4 How has she changed over the years?
5 Which two incidents in his past does she remind him of?
6 Why do you think her watch and clock stopped at twenty to nine?

Discussion

1 Can you remember anything that frightened you very much when you were a child? Try to explain why it was so frightening.

2 Everybody has 'expectations' of what life is going to be like. Miss Havisham expected to marry the man she loved, and was disappointed. Pip also has 'great expectations'. What about you? Describe your personal hopes and ambitions for the future.

Extension

Vocabulary

A A *veil* is a wedding head-dress. Write sentences explaining the following.

1 a bridegroom   4 the best man
2 a bride   5 a honeymoon
3 a bridesmaid

B *Satins, lace and silks* (line 5) are all *materials*. What are the following?

1 lamb, chicken, sausages, beef
2 carrots, potatoes, courgettes
3 sole, plaice, trout
4 iron, copper, tin
5 spanner, saw, hammer
6 oak, ash, beech
7 daisy, tulip, daffodil
8 lemons, apples, pears
9 table, bed, chair
10 butter, cream, cheese

C 'Some bright jewels sparkled on her neck' (line 7). Here are some more words connected with light: *glitter shine glow dazzle gleam*. Complete each sentence with the correct form of one of the words.

1 The wood in the fireplace was still .... although the flames had died down.
2 The frozen branches of the trees .... in the hard moonlight.
3 In the distance Fred saw a .... of light at the end of the tunnel.
4 We were very lucky. The sun .... every day of our holiday.
5 They were .... by the bright sunlight as they came out of the cinema.

Phrasal verbs

'Her watch and chain were not put on' (line 11). Complete each sentence so that it means the same as the one before, using a phrasal verb with *put*.

1 You can stay for the night at my parents' house. My parents can ....
2 We can't have our meeting this week, but next week will be OK. We'll have to ....
3 I know you don't like your job, but you can't change it at the moment. You'll just have to ....
4 I didn't feel like helping him, after he'd been so rude to me. His rudeness ....
5 I've got a suggestion to make. I'd like to ....
6 They've had central heating installed recently. They've had ....
7 You'll have to save enough to pay a deposit. You'll have to save enough ....
8 Did the operator connect you? Did the operator ....

Grammar

'I saw that everything within my view ... had been white long ago' (line 16). Use past simple and past perfect tenses to complete the sentences.

1 The hotel manager realized that the couple (leave) without paying their bill.
2 When Bill (arrive) home yesterday, he (find) the front door open.
3 I didn't recognize him, because I (not see) him before.
4 The teacher was angry because the class (not do) their homework.
5 I looked at Roger, and noticed that he (not shave) that morning.
6 Before he (set off) for the airport, he (phone) to check that the flight was on time.
7 I (bump) into Fenella last week. I (not see) her for years.
8 After she (go) round the museum, she (buy) some postcards.

Composition (120 – 180 words)

1 Imagine that you are a child of eight or nine years old. One winter evening last year, you were walking home from school, just as it was beginning to get dark. Suddenly, as you turned a corner, you saw a very strange sight. Describe what you saw, and your reaction.

2 You have recently been on a long train journey, when you had plenty of time to observe your fellow-passengers. Describe someone you noticed, who was dressed rather strangely, and try to imagine why he/she was dressed like that.

3 Imagine what happened on Miss Havisham's wedding day, all those years ago. Describe the preparations that were being made, and how she was feeling. Then, at twenty to nine, a letter was delivered to her. Write what you think happened next.

GEORGE ELIOT

1819 – 1880

Mary Ann or Marian Evans, who wrote under the pen-name of George Eliot, was born on a farm just outside Coventry in Warwickshire, England. She read widely and her teachers soon realized that she was exceptionally intelligent. After her mother's death in 1836 she had to run the house for her father and brother, but when her father died in 1849, she travelled in Europe with friends. She then moved to London, where she wrote articles for magazines, and met many leading literary figures. Her friends encouraged her to write fiction.

When she sent her first novel to her publisher, she used the name of George Eliot. However, when *Scenes of Clerical Life* was published in 1858, Charles Dickens realized at once that the writer was a woman. In addition, people in her home county of Warwickshire complained, because they recognized themselves in her carefully detailed descriptions.

George Eliot worked extremely hard on researching the backgrounds for her books. Her themes are varied, and much of her writing highlights the hypocrisy of Victorian society; there is often a moral conflict for her characters. George Eliot is well-known for her descriptions of country life (in *Silas Marner* and *Adam Bede*) and provincial life (in *Middlemarch*), but it is her remarkable imagination and intellectual power which make her one of the great English novelists. *Middlemarch* is generally considered her greatest work.

Well-known works by George Eliot include: *Scenes of Clerical Life* (1858), *Adam Bede* (1859), *The Mill on the Floss* (1860), *Silas Marner* (1861), *Romola* (1863), *Felix Holt* (1866), *Middlemarch* (1872), *Daniel Deronda* (1876).

Silas Marner

When Silas Marner, a linen-weaver, is falsely accused of stealing money in his home town, his fiancée breaks off their engagement and his friends abandon him. He moves to the village of Raveloe, and there, rejected and lonely, spends all his time and energy on his work. He is well paid for his weaving, and gradually the money he earns becomes his only interest in life. Every evening he counts his pile of gold coins, which he keeps under the floor in his cottage.

In this extract, Silas has just returned home, and is looking forward to eating some roast meat for his supper, for a change.

As soon as he was warm he began to think it would be a long while to wait till after supper before he drew out his guineas, and it would be pleasant to see them on the table before him as he ate his unwonted feast. For joy is the best of wine, and Silas's guineas were a golden wine of that sort.

5 He rose and placed his candle unsuspectingly on the floor near his loom, swept away the sand without noticing any change, and removed the bricks. The sight of the empty hole made his heart leap violently, but the belief that his gold was gone could not come at once – only terror, and the eager effort to put an end to the terror. He passed his trembling hand all about the hole, trying to think it possible that his eyes had

10 deceived him; then he held the candle in the hole and examined it curiously, trembling more and more.

At last he shook so violently that he let fall the candle, and lifted his hands to his head, trying to steady himself, that he might think. Had he put his gold somewhere else, by a sudden resolution last night, and then forgotten it? A man falling into dark waters

15 seeks a momentary footing even on sliding stones; and Silas, by acting as if he believed in false hopes, warded off the moment of despair. He searched in every corner, he turned his bed over, and shook it, and kneaded it; he looked in his brick oven where he laid his sticks. When there was no other place to be searched, he kneeled down again and felt once more all round the hole. There was no untried refuge left for a moment's

20 shelter from the terrible truth.

. . . . .

Silas got up from his knees trembling, and looked round at the table: didn't the gold lie there after all? The table was bare. Then he turned and looked behind him – looked all round his dwelling, seeming to strain his brown eyes after some possible appearance of the bags where he had already sought them in vain. He could see every object in his

25 cottage – and his gold was not there.

Again he put his trembling hands to his head, and gave a wild, ringing scream, the cry of desolation. For a few moments after he stood motionless; but the cry had relieved him from the first maddening pressure of the truth. He turned and tottered towards his loom, and got into the seat where he worked, instinctively seeking this as the strongest

30 assurance of reality.

And now that all the false hopes had vanished, and the first shock of certainty was past, the idea of a thief began to present itself, and he entertained it eagerly, because a thief might be caught and made to restore the gold.

Notes		
guineas: old gold coins	*strain his eyes after:* try too hard to see
unwonted: unusual	*desolation:* loneliness, despair
loom: a machine for weaving	*tottered:* walked with difficulty
seeks: looks for	*assurance:* a comforting reminder
warded off: pushed away	*entertained:* considered
no untried refuge: no other place to hide	*restore:* give back
dwelling: home	

Comprehension

The author

How much can you remember? Answer these questions quickly, without referring back to page 35.

1 George Eliot's real name was ....
2 She was born in the year ....
3 Her first novel was called ....
4 .... realized at once that George Eliot was a woman.
5 .... is usually considered her greatest work.
6 She died in the year ....

The text

A Match these words or phrases from the text with their meanings.

1 unsuspectingly (line 5) a not realizing anything was wrong
2 terror (line 8) b disappeared
3 eager (line 8) c shaking
4 trembling (line 9) d hopelessness
5 examined (line 10) e looked carefully at
6 resolution (line 14) f great fear
7 despair (line 16) g decision
8 relieved (line 27) h without thinking
9 instinctively (line 29) i keen, impatient
10 vanished (line 31) j made him feel better

B Rewrite these phrases or sentences in your own words.

1 he drew out his guineas (line 2)
2 his unwonted feast (line 3)
3 joy is the best of wine (line 3)
4 his eyes had deceived him (line 9)
5 he let fall the candle (line 12)
6 a moment's shelter from the terrible truth (line 19)
7 the table was bare (line 22)
8 he had already sought them in vain (line 24)

C Answer these questions.

1 When does Silas normally bring out his gold coins to count them?
2 Is Silas drinking wine with his supper? Can you explain the references to wine in the first paragraph?
3 Where does he usually keep his gold?
4 Does he realize at once that the gold has gone?
5 'A man falling into dark waters seeks a momentary footing even on sliding stones' (line 14). Can you explain this image with reference to Silas?
6 What are the 'false hopes' (line 16) Silas believes in for a few moments?
7 Where does Silas search for the gold?
8 What is 'the terrible truth' (line 20)?
9 What does Silas do when he realizes the truth?
10 Why is the loom such a comfort to him?

Discussion

1 Why is Silas so upset by the loss of his gold?
2 Is money important to you? Do you enjoy saving, or spending it? Do you have a budget? What do you spend money on?

Role-play

Students A and B: You are students who share a flat. You've had problems paying your bills and making your money last till the end of the term. Now you want to get organized, but you have different ideas.

Student A: You feel relaxed about money. You think you should have a 'kitty', i.e. you both contribute a large sum of money, and pay for everything out of that. When there isn't any left, you just put more money in the kitty.

Student B: You think the best way is to note down how much you both spend on everything, to see if you can cut down a bit. You are especially worried about the phone bill. (Student A has a lot of friends in other countries!)

Extension

Vocabulary

'(He) tottered towards his loom' (line 28). These are all words associated with walking: *stagger limp march trudge skip stroll*. Use them correctly in the following sentences.

1 He .... straight into the manager's office and demanded his money back.
2 Holding her head, she .... to the phone and called an ambulance.
3 I've twisted my ankle – that's why I'm ....
4 The two little girls .... happily round the garden.
5 I haven't got much to do after lunch, so I think I'll just .... down to the park.
6 Loaded down with shopping bags, she .... wearily all the way up the hill.

Grammar

'(He) got into the seat where he worked' (line 29). Complete each sentence with one of these relative pronouns: *where who which that whose*.

1 James has a wonderful teacher, ... patience is really incredible.
2 I think the writer .... won the Whitbread Prize has never had anything published before.
3 That's the house .... my aunt was born.
4 The only books .... were sold were thrillers.
5 The man .... fingerprints were taken by the police may have escaped.
6 We stayed at the hotel .... offered us the cheapest rooms.
7 He lives next door to the girl .... keeps appearing in instant coffee commercials.
8 In my opinion it's the best documentary on pollution .... has ever been made.

Confusing verbs

'Didn't the gold lie there ...' (line 21). Look carefully at these three verbs with different meanings: *lie/lied/lied   lie/lay/lain   lay/laid/laid*. Now use them correctly in these sentences.

1 The hen has .... two eggs every day this week.
2 I don't feel well. I'm going to .... down.
3 Could you .... the table for supper?
4 He's .... to you before, so why do you believe him?
5 When we're on holiday, we spend all our time .... on the beach.
6 The mayor .... the foundation stone for the new hospital.
7 Exhausted, he .... back in his favourite armchair.
8 The dog has been .... in front of the fire all evening.
9 Just imagine! This ancient vase has .... buried here in the sand for two thousand years!
10 He never tells the truth if he can avoid it. He enjoys ...., you see.

Composition (120 – 180 words)

1 You left your purse or wallet, with a lot of money in it, at a friend's house, by accident. When you remembered and went to look for it, it wasn't there. Describe your feelings, and what you did next.

2 'Money makes the world go round.' 'Money can't buy you love.' Which of these statements do you agree with? Explain your ideas.

3 Your favourite magazine is running a competition, with a prize of £5000 for the best article on how to spend £5000. Write the article you would enter for the competition, explaining exactly how you would spend the money.

9

ELIZABETH GASKELL

1810 – 1865

Elizabeth Cleghorn Stevenson was born in London, the daughter of a civil servant, but as her mother died very soon after her birth, she was brought up by an aunt in Cheshire. She married William Gaskell, a church minister in Manchester, when she was 22. With her husband and four daughters she led a happy, busy life in Manchester, interested in all the social, political and religious matters of the time.

When her only son died young, Elizabeth Gaskell started writing in order to express her feelings of sorrow. She had great success with her first novel, *Mary Barton*, in which she gives a harsh but realistic portrayal of working people's lives in Manchester, and she went on to produce five more novels, and various short stories. *Cranford* is perhaps her most popular work, and is set in Knutsford, the small town where she grew up.

Features of Elizabeth Gaskell's writing are her subtle descriptions of character and her delicate irony. Charles Dickens published some of her work in the magazines he edited, and she was a close friend of Charlotte Brontë. In fact, when Charlotte Brontë died, Elizabeth Gaskell wrote a truthful yet sympathetic biography of her friend, which has remained a classic. Her finest work, however, is generally considered to be *Wives and Daughters*.

Well-known works by Elizabeth Gaskell are *Mary Barton* (1848), *Cranford* (1853), *Ruth* (1853), *North and South* (1855), *The Life of Charlotte Brontë* (1857), *Sylvia's Lovers* (1863), *Wives and Daughters* (1866).

Wives and Daughters

This was Elizabeth Gaskell's last novel, which was not quite finished when she died. It is set in the town of Hollingford, which is based on Knutsford.

Mr Gibson is a hard-working doctor, a widower who lives simply but happily with his young daughter Molly. However, he considers that he should remarry, partly to give Molly a stepmother's care. He feels attracted towards a pretty widow, Mrs Kirkpatrick. She works as a governess in an aristocratic family (who call her by her maiden surname, Clare), but she would love to find another husband and give up her job. She also has a daughter, called Cynthia.

In this conversation, the doctor and Mrs Kirkpatrick come to an important decision.

'Cynthia seems to me such an out-of-the-way name, only fit for poetry, not for daily use.'

'It is mine,' said Mrs Kirkpatrick, in a plaintive tone of reproach. 'I was christened Hyacinth, and her poor father would have her called after me. I'm sorry you don't like it.'

Mr Gibson did not know what to say. He was not quite prepared to plunge into the directly personal style. While he was hesitating, she went on:

'Hyacinth Clare! Once upon a time I was quite proud of my pretty name; and other people thought it pretty, too.'

'I've no doubt –' Mr Gibson began; and then stopped.

'Perhaps I did wrong in yielding to his wish, to have her called by such a romantic name. It may excite prejudice against her in some people; and, poor child! she will have enough to struggle with. A young daughter is a great charge, Mr Gibson, especially when there is only one parent to look after her.'

'You are quite right,' said he, recalled to the remembrance of Molly; 'though I should have thought that a girl who is so fortunate as to have a mother could not feel the loss of her father so acutely as one who is motherless must suffer from her deprivation.'

'You are thinking of your own daughter. It was careless of me to say what I did. Dear child! How well I remember her sweet little face as she lay sleeping on my bed. I suppose she is nearly grown-up now. She must be near my Cynthia's age. How I should like to see her!'

'I hope you will. I should like you to see her. I should like you to love my poor little Molly – to love her as your own –' He swallowed down something that rose in his throat, and was nearly choking him.

'Is he going to offer? Is he?' she wondered; and she began to tremble in the suspense before he next spoke.

'Could you love her as your daughter? Will you try? Will you give me the right of introducing you to her as her future mother; as my wife?'

There! he had done it – whether it was wise or foolish – he had done it! but he was aware that the question as to its wisdom came into his mind the instant that the words were said past recall.

She hid her face in her hands.

'Oh! Mr Gibson,' she said; and then, a little to his surprise, and a great deal to her own, she burst into hysterical tears: it was such a wonderful relief to feel that she need not struggle any more for a livelihood.

'My dear – my dearest,' said he, trying to soothe her with word and caress; but, just at the moment, uncertain what name he ought to use. After her sobbing had abated a little, she said herself, as if understanding his difficulty:

'Call me Hyacinth – your own Hyacinth. I can't bear 'Clare'. It does so remind me of being a governess, and those days are all past now.'

> **Notes**
> *plaintive:* sad, complaining
> *reproach:* blame
> *christened:* given the name (at a religious ceremony)
> *Hyacinth:* the name of a flower with a strong scent, a very unusual girl's name
> *plunge into:* go suddenly into
> *struggle:* fight, work hard
> *a great charge:* a great responsibility
> *acutely:* sharply, bitterly
> *deprivation:* loss
>
> *choking him:* making it difficult for him to breathe
> *to offer:* (here) to ask her to marry him
> *suspense:* wondering what will happen
> *hysterical:* wild, uncontrolled
> *livelihood:* a way of earning money to live on
> *soothe:* calm, quieten
> *caress:* gentle touching
> *sobbing:* loud crying, weeping
> *abated:* become quieter
> *governess:* a woman who teaches children in their home

Comprehension

The author

Complete these sentences in your own words.

1 Elizabeth Gaskell was brought up by ....
2 After she married, she lived in ....
3 Her life there with her family was ....
4 She started writing because ....
5 Because she was a friend of Charlotte Brontë, ...

The text

A Rewrite the following phrases or sentences in your own words.

1 her poor father would have her called after me (line 4)
2 yielding to his wish (line 11)
3 excite prejudice against her (line 12)
4 she will have enough to struggle with (line 12)
5 recalled to the remembrance of Molly (line 15)
6 to love her as your own (line 23)
7 the words were said past recall (line 30)
8 those days are all past now (line 40)

B Answer these questions.

1 Mrs Kirkpatrick's name is Hyacinth. Can you explain why she says that Cynthia is her name?
2 Why does Mr Gibson hesitate (line 7)?
3 Who do you think the 'other people' are, who thought Hyacinth's name was pretty?

4 'A young daughter is a great charge, Mr Gibson' (line 13). Do you think Mrs Kirkpatrick has any secret motive for saying this? What effect does this statement have on Mr Gibson?
5 Who does Mr Gibson think is more important in a young girl's life, a mother or a father?
6 'Dear child! How well I remember her sweet little face' (line 18). Do you think Mrs Kirkpatrick is sincere in her praise of Molly? Is her enthusiasm motivated by politeness, or something else?
7 How do you know from the text that Mrs Kirkpatrick is very anxious for Mr Gibson to propose marriage to her?
8 What question comes into Mr Gibson's mind as soon as he has proposed?
9 Why does Mrs Kirkpatrick 'burst into hysterical tears' (line 34)?
10 Why is Mr Gibson uncertain about what to call her?
11 Why doesn't Mrs Kirkpatrick want to be called Clare, the name she is known by at the moment?

Discussion

1 Mrs Kirkpatrick is delighted because now 'she need not struggle any more for a livelihood' (line 34). How would you feel if you did not have to work for a living? What are the advantages and disadvantages of having to work? What would you do every day if you didn't have to go to school or work? Discuss how you would spend your time.

2 Mrs Kirkpatrick cleverly directs the conversation to encourage Mr Gibson to propose marriage to her. In an indirect way she persuades him to offer to marry her. Do you think this is fair? Does Mr Gibson realize what is happening? Do you think he will reconsider his offer, or perhaps go ahead and marry her, but regret it later?

Role-play

Student A: You want to persuade your friend (Student B) to go to the cinema/get tickets for a concert/watch a football match with you. Use every possible argument to persuade him/her.

Student B: You are not interested in any of your friend's suggestions, because you are too tired/short of money/not keen on football. Try not to let yourself be persuaded.

Extension

Word-building

'It may excite prejudice' (line 12). *Excite* is a verb, the related noun is *excitement*, and the adjective is *exciting*. Fill in the gaps in the table.

	verb	noun	adjective
1	remember	......	memorable
2	pride	......	proud
3	doubt	......	......
4	lose	......	......
5	surprise	......	......
6	x	......	wise
7	hesitate	......	hesitant

Conjunctions

'Though I should have thought ...' (line 15). These words have a similar meaning but take different grammatical constructions: *although however despite but*. Put them into the correct sentences.

1 I gave him the information. ...., he did not make good use of it.
2 She may not be good at maths, ... she's a wonderful swimmer.
3 .... the rain, we all went for a long walk.
4 .... he had had very few lessons, he passed his driving test first time.
5 I didn't really want to go to the conference, ... my boss talked me into it.
6 .... he had saved up a lot of money, it still wasn't enough to buy the CD-player he wanted.
7 She takes part in several sports, ... being severely handicapped.
8 Cycling is a good way of beating traffic jams. ...., there are dangers involved in this type of transport.

Phrasal verbs

'While he was hesitating, she went on' (line 7). Complete these sentences with the correct form of a phrasal verb with *go*.

1 Last night another bomb .... in the city centre.
2 Inflation .... again last month.
3 I don't think those brown shoes .... that blue suit.
4 Just tell me what's .... here, will you!
5 The teacher .... the exercise again, and finally the pupils understood.
6 Philip was very nervous about asking Julia to .... with him.
7 Time .... so slowly that she couldn't believe it was still the same day.

Composition (120 – 180 words)

Imagine that you are Mrs Kirkpatrick, writing to tell your best friend the wonderful news of your engagement to Mr Gibson. Write the letter in informal style.

10

WILKIE COLLINS

1824 – 1889

William Wilkie Collins was born in London, the son of a painter. He worked for a tea importer, and later studied law, but never worked as a lawyer. He was a close friend and colleague of Charles Dickens from 1851 to Dickens' death. He wrote numerous articles and short stories for magazines edited by Dickens, but is best known for his novels. Although he lived in London, he travelled widely in France and Italy, often with Dickens.

In his writing Wilkie Collins was an expert at mystery, suspense and crime. He wrote the first full-length detective stories in English, and many modern detective-story writers base their technique on his. *The Woman in White* and *The Moonstone* are his most famous novels. The poet T. S. Eliot called *The Moonstone* 'the first, the longest and the best of modern detective novels'. Collins specialized in constructing clever, carefully detailed plots, and he always checked his facts meticulously.

Well-known works by Wilkie Collins include: *Basil* (1852), *The Woman in White* (1860), *No Name* (1862), *Armadale* (1866), *The Moonstone* (1868).

The Moonstone

The Moonstone is a beautiful, priceless diamond, which was originally stolen from a religious temple in India, and brought to England. Its Indian guardians have followed it and are intent on taking it back. It is now in the possession of an English family, and is soon to be given to Miss Rachel Verinder on her eighteenth birthday.

The Verinders live in a large country house, and their old butler, Gabriel, is telling the story. His daughter, Penelope, also a servant in the house, has recently seen some Indian jugglers in the village, performing tricks with a bottle of ink. Gabriel wants to make sure that no thieves enter the house.

Towards midnight, I went round the house to lock up, accompanied by my second in command (Samuel, the footman), as usual. When all the doors were made fast, except the side door that opened on the terrace, I sent Samuel to bed, and stepped out for a breath of fresh air before I too went to bed in my turn.

5   The night was still and close, and the moon was at the full in the heavens. It was so silent out of doors that I heard from time to time, very faint and low, the fall of the sea, as the ground-swell heaved it in on the sand-bank near the mouth of our little bay. As the house stood, the terrace side was the dark side; but the broad moonlight showed fair on the gravel walk that ran along the next side to the terrace. Looking this way, after

10   looking up at the sky, I saw the shadow of a person in the moonlight thrown forward from behind the corner of the house.

Being old and sly, I forbore to call out; but being also, unfortunately, old and heavy, my feet betrayed me on the gravel. Before I could steal suddenly round the corner, as I had proposed, I heard lighter feet than mine – and more than one pair of them as I

15   thought – retreating in a hurry. By the time I had got to the corner, the trespassers, whoever they were, had run into the shrubbery at the off side of the walk, and were hidden from sight among the thick trees and bushes in that part of the grounds. From the shrubbery, they could easily make their way, over our fence, into the road. If I had been forty years younger, I might have had a chance of catching them before they got

20   clear of our premises. As it was, I went back to set a-going a younger pair of legs than mine. Without disturbing anybody, Samuel and I got a couple of guns, and went all round the house and through the shrubbery. Having made sure that no persons were lurking about anywhere in our grounds, we turned back. Passing over the walk where I had seen the shadow, I now noticed, for the first time, a little bright object lying on the

25   clean gravel, under the light of the moon. Picking the object up, I discovered it was a small bottle, containing a thick sweet-smelling liquor, as black as ink.

I said nothing to Samuel. But, remembering what Penelope had told me about the jugglers, and the pouring of the little pool of ink into the palm of the boy's hand, I instantly suspected that I had disturbed the three Indians, lurking about the house, and

30   bent, in their heathenish way, on discovering the whereabouts of the Diamond that night.

Notes	
second in command: an assistant (usually in the army or navy)	*trespassers:* strangers who have no right to be there
footman: a (male) servant	*shrubbery:* groups of small trees and bushes
close: (here) warm and airless	*off side:* other side
ground-swell: slow-moving waves	*premises:* land, grounds
showed fair: shone brightly	*set a-going:* (old-fashioned) start moving
gravel: small stones	*persons:* people
walk: a path	*liquor:* (old-fashioned) liquid
sly: clever, cunning	*jugglers:* people who do clever tricks by throwing things into the air and catching them
forbore to: stopped myself from	*heathenish:* (old-fashioned) not Christian

Comprehension

The author

Only one ending in each group is correct. Choose the correct one.

1 Wilkie Collins worked
  a as a painter.
  b for a tea company.
  c as a lawyer.

2 He was very good at
  a inventing complicated plots.
  b describing a famous detective.
  c writing about real crimes.

3 He travelled a lot
  a in India.
  b with his wife.
  c in Europe.

4 He is best known for his
  a short stories.
  b novel *The Moonstone*.
  c friendship with Dickens.

The text

A Match these words from the text with their meanings.

1 still (line 5)   a pushed
2 heavens (line 5)   b not visible, concealed
3 faint (line 6)   c quiet, without movement
4 heaved (line 7)   d sky
5 hidden (line 17)   e immediately
6 instantly (line 29)   f soft

B Rewrite these phrases or sentences in your own words.

1 all the doors were made fast (line 2)
2 my feet betrayed me on the gravel (line 13)
3 steal suddenly (line 13)

4 as I had proposed (line 13)
5 retreating in a hurry (line 15)
6 a younger pair of legs than mine (line 20)
7 lurking about (line 23)
8 bent ... on discovering the whereabouts of (line 30)

C Answer these questions.

1 Who normally goes round the house to lock up?
2 Why does Gabriel leave the side door open?
3 What does Gabriel see in the moonlight?
4 What do you know about Gabriel's physical shape and condition?
5 How many 'trespassers' do you think there are?
6 Where do they hide, and how do they escape?
7 Why does Gabriel get Samuel to help him?
8 What clue does Gabriel find on the gravel?
9 Why does he suspect that the trespassers are Indians?
10 What does he think they are looking for?

Discussion

1 What do you think will happen next? Will the Indians manage to get back the Moonstone?

2 The Indians probably think that 'the end justifies the means'. Do you think it is right to do something illegal or immoral for a good reason?

Role-play

Student A: You have just received an expensive new mountain bike for your birthday and are delighted with it. Your friend (Student B) wants to borrow it. Say no tactfully, explaining how valuable it is.

Student B: You think Student A is being rather mean. You only want to borrow the bike for a day at the weekend, and you often used to lend him/her *your* old bike. Explain how careful you will be with it, and why you want to borrow it. Persuade him/her to agree.

Extension

Similes

'As black as ink' (line 26). Match the adjectives on the left with the nouns on the right, to produce common similes.

1	deaf	a	a picture
2	good	b	pie
3	old	c	a church mouse
4	dry	d	a post
5	fresh	e	a daisy
6	poor	f	gold
7	easy	g	dust
8	pretty	h	the hills

Grammar

A 'If I had been forty years younger, I might have had a chance of catching them' (line 18). Make third conditional sentences about these past situations.

1 He didn't tell the truth, so I didn't believe him.
2 I couldn't speak Russian, so they didn't offer me the job.
3 He was given a life sentence because he hadn't shown any compassion for his victims.
4 I got the sum wrong because I didn't use my calculator.
5 They didn't buy the cottage because it was too far from the main road.
6 You didn't say you were sorry, so I couldn't forgive you.
7 She didn't follow the recipe, so the cake turned out badly.
8 When he married her, he didn't know how selfish she was.
9 I should have tried acupuncture treatment to stop smoking.
10 I didn't realize I was supposed to wear a suit to the office.

B 'Lighter feet than mine...' (line 14). Give the correct comparatives for the following adjectives.

1	comfortable	11	modern
2	easy	12	clever
3	rich	13	heavy
4	difficult	14	beautiful
5	happy	15	friendly
6	intelligent	16	good
7	ugly	17	educational
8	flexible	18	bad
9	slow	19	fast
10	thin	20	far

C 'Lighter feet than mine...' (line 14). Complete these sentences with either *than* or *then*.

1 I paid the bill, ... I left the restaurant.
2 She's much more efficient .... our last secretary.
3 Your house is nearer .... mine, isn't it?
4 First you turn the key, ... you press the button.
5 Just ...., a tall dark man came in.
6 I'd rather have tea .... coffee, please.
7 No sooner had the bell rung .... all the pupils rushed out.

Composition (120 – 180 words)

1 Describe in detail a very valuable object that you have seen, perhaps in a museum. How was it protected from theft?
2 Write a formal letter to your insurance company, explaining when and how your watch/bicycle/computer was stolen. Give a detailed description of the stolen object.
3 Write an informal letter to a friend, describing how something was stolen from you recently, and how you are managing without it until you can get a replacement.

11

THOMAS HARDY

1840 – 1928

Thomas Hardy was born in Higher Bockhampton in Dorset, England, and grew up surrounded by rural traditions. His father was a stonemason, and Hardy studied church restoration. While working as an architect in London, he began writing – first poetry, and then novels. After the success of *Far From the Madding Crowd*, he felt able to marry. Eventually the Hardys had a house built in Dorset, where they lived for the rest of their lives.

By the time his wife died in 1912, Hardy had published all his major novels and was a famous, well-loved poet and novelist. He expressed his feelings of guilt and regret at her death in his poetry. He married again, and died at the age of 87.

Some critics maintain that his novels are Hardy's greatest achievement, while others attach more importance to his poetry. Most of his novels are set in his native Dorset (called Wessex), and they all reflect his love for the countryside. Farming techniques and country customs are described in careful, loving detail. Hardy was aware that progress, in the form of advanced technology, would soon change these for ever.

Like many country people, Hardy was a fatalist, believing that people must simply accept whatever happens in life. However, he disapproved of the strict code of moral behaviour which existed in his time, which did not allow for human feelings or mistakes. His books are read today for their great themes of love and tragedy, and for their beautiful descriptions of the English countryside as it used to be.

Well-known works by Thomas Hardy include: *Under the Greenwood Tree* (1872), *Far From the Madding Crowd* (1874), *The Return of the Native* (1878), *The Mayor of Casterbridge* (1886), *Tess of the D'Urbervilles* (1891), *Jude the Obscure* (1895).

Far From the Madding Crowd

This book was a turning point for Hardy, and marks the beginning of his successful literary career.

Bathsheba Everdene, a beautiful, independent young woman, comes to live with her aunt in a Dorset village. Gabriel Oak, a young farmer, has seen her several times and is greatly attracted to her. By chance she saves Oak's life, and in this extract he introduces himself.

'I believe you saved my life, Miss – I don't know your name. I know your aunt's, but not yours.'

'I would just as soon not tell it – rather not. There is no reason either why I should, as you probably will never have much to do with me.'

'Still I should like to know.'

'You can inquire at my aunt's – she will tell you.'

'My name is Gabriel Oak.'

'And mine isn't. You seem fond of yours in speaking it so decisively, Gabriel Oak.'

'You see, it is the only one I shall ever have, and I must make the most of it.'

'I always think mine sounds odd and disagreeable.'

'I should think you might soon get a new one.'

'Mercy! – how many opinions you keep about you concerning other people, Gabriel Oak.'

'Well, Miss – excuse the words – I thought you would like them. But I can't match you, I know, in mapping out my mind upon my tongue. I never was very clever in my inside. But I thank you. Come, give me your hand!'

She hesitated, somewhat disconcerted at Oak's old-fashioned earnest conclusion to a dialogue lightly carried on. 'Very well,' she said, and gave him her hand, compressing her lips to a demure impassivity. He held it but an instant, and in his fear of being too demonstrative, swerved to the opposite extreme, touching her fingers with the lightness of a small-hearted person.

'I am sorry,' he said the instant after.

'What for?'

'Letting go your hand so quick.'

'You may have it again if you like; there it is.' She gave him her hand again.

Oak held it longer this time – indeed, curiously long. 'How soft it is – being winter time, too – not chapped or rough, or anything!' he said.

'There – that's long enough,' said she, though without pulling it away. 'But I suppose you are thinking you would like to kiss it? You may if you want to.'

'I wasn't thinking of any such thing,' said Gabriel simply; 'but I will – .'

'That you won't!' She snatched back her hand. 'Now find out my name,' she said teasingly; and withdrew.

Notes *Mercy!:* (exclamation) Well!, My goodness!	*swerved:* moved
hesitated: couldn't decide for a moment	*chapped:* cracked and sore
disconcerted: confused	*snatched back:* pulled away quickly
demure: modest	*teasingly:* playfully
demonstrative: showing much affection	*withdrew:* went away

Comprehension

The author

Only one sentence in each group is correct. Choose the correct one.

1 a Hardy grew up in London.
  b He studied architecture in London.
  c He started writing in London.

2 a He lived with his first wife in London and Dorset.
  b He was happy when she died.
  c He married three times altogether.

3 a He hoped that machines would soon take the place of farm labourers.
  b He understood country life very well.
  c He thought that people should take responsibility for their own lives.

The text

A Match these words from the text with their meanings.

1 decisively (line 8)   a confidently
2 disagreeable (line 10)   b serious
3 somewhat (line 17)   c unpleasant
4 earnest (line 17)   d calmness
5 dialogue (line 18)   e rather
6 impassivity (line 19)   f strangely
7 curiously (line 26)   g conversation

B Rewrite these phrases or sentences in your own words.

1 I can't match you (line 14)
2 mapping out my mind upon my tongue (line 15)
3 I never was very clever in my inside (line 15)
4 a dialogue lightly carried on (line 18)
5 compressing her lips (line 18)
6 but an instant (line 19)
7 swerved to the opposite extreme (line 20)
8 a small-hearted person (line 21)

C Answer these questions.

1 What reason does Bathsheba give for not telling Oak her name?
2 What do you think Oak means when he says 'I should think you might soon get a new one' (line 11)?
3 Why does Bathsheba hesitate before giving Oak her hand (line 17)?
4 Why does Oak let go of her hand so quickly?
5 Oak says her hand is soft (line 26). Why is he surprised by this?

Discussion

1 What do you think finally happens in the book? Does Bathsheba marry Oak? Or does she fall in love with someone else?

2 How important is the name of a character or the title of a book? What do you think 'far from the madding crowd' means? And why did Hardy choose the names 'Oak' and 'Bathsheba' for his hero and heroine? Do these names have any special meaning?

3 Do you think women should keep their names when they marry? Should children have their father's or mother's family name, or both?

Extension

Vocabulary

'How soft it is!' (line 26). The opposite of *soft* is *hard*. Find opposites to these adjectives.

1 sharp (a knife)   5 tight (clothes)
2 smooth (skin)   6 guilty (a person)
3 tender (meat)   7 generous (a person)
4 confident (a person) 8 noisy (a child)

Expressions

'I must make the most of it' (line 9). Match these expressions with *make* with their definitions.

1 make a decision   a cause problems
2 make do   b earn a lot of money
3 make a fuss   c decide to do something
4 make a fortune   d complain, make a lot of
                            noise
5 make trouble   e give a talk
6 make a speech   f manage with whatever is
                            available

Punctuation

'I know your aunt's, but not yours' (line 1). Use the correct punctuation in these sentences.

1 wheres the teachers room please I want to see mr jones and miss green
2 the mountains not in tibet its in nepal
3 five oranges please and two apples
4 the cat drank its milk
5 hes a friend of johns isnt he
6 you shouldnt have taken his pens
7 its time we did some work in michaels garden
8 the students bags were lying on the floor where theyd left them

Grammar

'Letting go your hand so quick' (line 24). Oak is a countryman who does not always speak correctly. In standard English we would say *so quickly*, using the adverb, not the adjective. Give the adverbs for the following adjectives.

1 slow   5 automatic
2 angry   6 good
3 comfortable   7 beautiful
4 fast   8 hard

Prepositions

'You seem fond of yours' (line 8). Complete these sentences with the correct prepositions.

1   He's capable .... better work.
2   She's afraid .... the dark.
3   They're worried .... their future.
4   I'm satisfied .... your explanation.
5   She's married .... my best friend.
6   We're ready .... lunch.
7   I'm bad .... maths.
8   They're aware .... the problem.
9   He's proud .... his son.
10 That's typical .... her.
11 We're anxious .... our parents.
12 He's angry .... his sister.
13 They're related .... the Shakespeare family.
14 She's good .... skiing.

Composition (120 – 180 words)

1 Write a character description of the two people in the story so far.

2 Write a short article for a teenagers' magazine, using the title *Romance in the Air*. Give tips on making a good first impression, finding out someone's name and asking him/her out for the first time.

3 Write a description of your ideal husband or wife.

12

MARK TWAIN

1835 – 1910

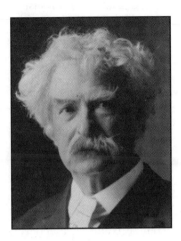

Samuel Langhorne Clemens was an American who wrote under the pen-name Mark Twain. His childhood and youth were spent in Hannibal, Missouri, a small town on the banks of the great Mississippi river. He left school at the age of twelve, and tried a variety of jobs, including that of river pilot, before finally becoming a journalist. As a reporter, he travelled widely, and began to publish the humorous, observant writing which made him famous.

Twain married in 1870, and moved to New England. He was a partner in a publishing company which did well for several years, but unwise investments led to his bankruptcy in 1894. Now began a period of exceedingly hard work to clear his debts, and his writing began to show signs of pessimism, which continued until his death.

Although he was well known in his lifetime for his satirical works, Mark Twain is most famous nowadays for his two classics of childhood experience, *Tom Sawyer* and *Huckleberry Finn*. In these novels he expresses the conflict between childhood and the adult world, between nature and civilization, between freedom and laws. He describes moments of violence and terror in a child's life, as well as perfect happiness, in a direct, vivid style, which had a powerful influence on later American writers.

Well-known works by Mark Twain include: *The Innocents Abroad* (1869), *The Adventures of Tom Sawyer* (1876), *The Adventures of Huckleberry Finn* (1884).

The Adventures of Tom Sawyer

Mark Twain said of this book 'Most of the adventures recorded in this book really occurred; one or two were experiences of my own, the rest those of boys who were schoolmates of mine.' His aim was 'to remind adults of what they once were themselves, and how they felt and thought and talked.'

Tom Sawyer, a young boy in a small American town, is constantly in trouble with the adults around him. In this extract we see him playing his greatest trick so far on the adult world. He has run away from home with his friends Huckleberry Finn (an orphan) and Joe Harper. For several days they have been sleeping on an island in the river. Their families have come to the sad conclusion that the boys must have drowned, and have arranged their funeral. Tom, Huck and Joe choose this moment to return.

The bell began to toll, instead of ringing in the usual way. It was a very still Sabbath, and the mournful sound seemed in keeping with the musing hush that lay upon nature. The villagers began to gather, loitering a moment in the vestibule to converse in whispers about the sad event. But there was no whispering in the house; only the
5 funereal rustling of dresses, as the women gathered to their seats, disturbed the silence there. None could remember when the little church had been so full before. There was finally a waiting pause, an expectant dumbness, and then Aunt Polly entered, followed by Sid and Mary, and then by the Harper family, all in deep black, and the whole congregation, the old minister as well, rose reverently and stood, until the mourners
10 were seated in the front pew. There was another communing silence, broken at intervals by muffled sobs, and then the minister spread his hands abroad and prayed. A moving hymn was sung, and the text followed: 'I am the resurrection and the life.'

As the service proceeded, the clergyman drew such pictures of the graces, the winning ways, and the rare promise of the lost lads, that every soul there, thinking he
15 recognized these pictures, felt a pang in remembering that he had persistently blinded himself to them always before, and had as persistently seen only faults and flaws in the poor boys. The minister related many a touching incident in the lives of the departed, too, which illustrated their sweet, generous natures, and the people could easily see, now, how noble and beautiful those episodes were, and remembered with grief that at
20 the time they occurred they had seemed rank rascalities, well deserving of the cowhide. The congregation became more and more moved as the pathetic tale went on, till at last the whole company broke down and joined the weeping mourners in a chorus of anguished sobs, the preacher himself giving way to his feelings, and crying in the pulpit.

There was a rustle in the gallery which nobody noticed; a moment later the church
25 door creaked; the minister raised his streaming eyes above his handkerchief, and stood transfixed! First one and then another pair of eyes followed the minister's, and then, almost with one impulse, the congregation rose and stared while the three dead boys came marching up the aisle, Tom in the lead, Joe next, and Huck, a ruin of drooping rags, sneaking sheepishly in the rear. They had been hid in the unused gallery, listening
30 to their own funeral sermon!

Aunt Polly, Mary, and the Harpers threw themselves upon their restored ones, smothered them with kisses and poured out thanksgivings, while poor Huck stood abashed and uncomfortable, not knowing exactly what to do or where to hide from so many unwelcoming eyes. He wavered, and started to slink away, but Tom seized him
35 and said:

'Aunt Polly, it ain't fair. Somebody's got to be glad to see Huck.'

'And so they shall! I'm glad to see him, poor motherless thing!' And the loving attentions Aunt Polly lavished upon him were the one thing capable of making him even more uncomfortable than he was before.

Notes *toll:* to ring slowly, for a death	*minister, clergyman:* priest

Notes

toll: to ring slowly, for a death
Sabbath: Sunday
musing hush: thoughtful silence
loitering: stopping, waiting
vestibule: hall, porch
funereal: sad (as at a funeral)
congregation: people attending church
mourners: family and friends at a funeral
pew: a row of seats in a church
muffled sobs: quiet crying
abroad: (here) wide
moving: emotional, sad
'I am the resurrection and the life': a text from the Bible

minister, clergyman: priest
winning: (here) charming
touching: causing sympathy
rank rascalities: wicked deeds
cowhide: (here) a whip
pulpit: a raised platform for the priest
aisle: space between the seats in the centre of the church
sermon: a talk given by the priest
smothered: covered
abashed: embarrassed
slink: to move so that no one notices
it ain't fair: (ungrammatical) it isn't fair

Comprehension

The author

Correct these sentences if necessary. Tick any sentences which are already correct.

1 Mark Twain lived all his life in Hannibal, Missouri.
2 He studied journalism at university.
3 He became famous for his scientific writing.
4 He never married.
5 His style of writing remained cheerful and optimistic until his death.

The text

A Match these words or phrases from the text with their meanings.

1 still (line 1)   a very sad
2 mournful (line 2)   b talk
3 converse (line 3)   c with determination
4 reverently (line 9)   d respectfully
5 at intervals (line 10) e quiet, with no wind
6 persistently (line 15) f hesitated
7 the departed (line 17) g crying
8 weeping (line 22)   h occasionally
9 restored (line 31)   i the dead
10 wavered (line 34)   j given back

B Find three phrases that refer to the boys' good qualities, and two nouns that refer to their character defects.

C Rewrite these phrases or sentences in your own words.

1 every soul there ... felt a pang (line 14)
2 well deserving of the cowhide (line 20)
3 a chorus of anguished sobs (line 22)
4 the minister ... stood transfixed (line 25)
5 Huck, a ruin of drooping rags (line 28)
6 sneaking sheepishly (line 29)
7 poured out thanksgivings (line 32)
8 the loving attentions Aunt Polly lavished upon him (line 37)

D Answer these questions.

1 Why is the boys' funeral taking place?
2 Why do the congregation have a very different opinion of the boys now that they are understood to be dead?
3 What is the atmosphere like in the church?
4 What is the reaction of the families when the boys come 'marching up the aisle'?
5 Why doesn't anybody welcome Huck at first?
6 Do Aunt Polly's 'loving attentions' make him feel better?

Discussion

1 Do you think it was wrong of the boys to play such a trick on their families and the village people? How do you think the congregation will feel later – happy that the boys are alive, or angry at being deceived?

2 The reader knows that the boys are alive. Does this make the scene in the church more amusing, because we know something which the congregation are unaware of? Do you think it is a funny situation, or not?

Extension

Vocabulary

'The whole congregation' (line 8). Use the following nouns (for groups of people) correctly in the sentences below: *jury audience spectators viewers congregation staff team delegates.*

1 The conference .... greeted the speaker with rapturous applause.

2 Some of the .... expressed their disapproval of the play by walking out of the theatre at the interval, and demanding a refund.

3 The .... came back into court to give their verdict.

4 He always goes to watch his .... play their away matches, even if they're at the other end of the country.

5 Feel free to ask any member of ...., if you have any further queries.

6 We would like to ask .... not to adjust their television sets. There is some temporary interference.

7 At the end of the church service, the .... streamed out into the sunshine.

8 Most .... at football matches in Britain used to stand, but now there are many all-seater stadiums.

Animal expressions

'Sneaking sheepishly' (line 29). Complete each sentence with one of these animal names: *worm horse rat wolf dog cat fish.*

1 Poor man! He leads a ....'s life!

2 He tried to .... his way into a position of power, but failed.

3 My room's tiny! There isn't room to swing a ....!

4 I can't possibly come to your meeting. I have other .... to fry.

5 I hope we've bought enough food. He eats like a ....!

6 That seems very suspicious to me. I smell a ....!

7 Nobody believes him now, because he's cried .... too often.

Grammar

'A moving hymn was sung' (line 11). Put these active sentences into the passive, including the agent where necessary.

1 His father gave him a bicycle for his birthday.

2 Workmen are painting the flat next door.

3 Nobody has discovered a cure for the common cold yet.

4 People say that you shouldn't eat too much salt.

5 Nobody has lived in that house for years.

6 People consume a lot of ice-cream in hot weather.

7 Someone will meet you at the airport.

8 The authorities are going to build the bypass as planned.

Composition (120 – 180 words)

Imagine what other kinds of adventures Tom Sawyer and his friends might have. Write a story describing one of them, beginning *One day Tom and his friends were feeling bored ...*

13

HENRY JAMES

1843 – 1916

Henry James was born in New York City. His father and elder brother were well-known philosophers. He went to school in New York, London, Paris and Geneva, and studied law at Harvard University. He began to write brilliant reviews and short stories for American magazines, and after spending a year in Paris, where he met many famous literary figures, he settled in England and continued writing. He became a British citizen in 1915.

James wrote more than a hundred short stories, including the famous ghost story *The Turn of the Screw*, as well as plays, criticism, autobiography, travel books and many novels. His work as a novelist falls into three main periods, with different themes: firstly, the impact on American life of European civilization, secondly, English social, political and artistic life and, lastly, a return to the international theme.

James is renowned for his mastery of the psychological novel, which has had an important influence on later writers. In his writing he hardly ever concentrates on plot, but rather on character description and the apparently insignificant details which contribute to the whole portrayal.

Well-known works by Henry James include *Roderick Hudson* (1875), *The American* (1877), *Daisy Miller* (1878), *Washington Square* (1881), *The Portrait of a Lady* (1881), *The Bostonians* (1886), *The Wings of the Dove* (1902), *The Ambassadors* (1903), *The Golden Bowl* (1904).

Washington Square

This book, set in New York, belongs to Henry James's early period. Catherine Sloper lives in Washington Square with her widowed father, a rich doctor. She is shy and rather plain, and finds it difficult to make conversation or meet strangers. Dr Sloper is a little disappointed that his daughter is not as beautiful or as intelligent as her dead mother. Catherine will inherit his considerable wealth.

In this extract, at a fashionable dance, Catherine's cousin Marian has just introduced her to a very handsome young man, who has been asking to meet her.

Catherine was always agitated by an introduction; it seemed a difficult moment, and she wondered that some people – her new acquaintance at this moment, for instance – should mind it so little. She wondered what she ought to say, and what would be the consequences of her saying nothing. The consequences at present were very agreeable. Mr Townsend, leaving her no time for embarrassment, began to talk to her with an easy smile, as if he had known her for a year.

'What a delightful party! What a charming house! What an interesting family! What a pretty girl your cousin is!'

• • • • •

He looked straight into Catherine's eyes. She answered nothing; she only listened, and looked at him; and he, as if he expected no particular reply, went on to say many other things in the same comfortable and natural manner. Catherine, though she felt tongue-tied, was conscious of no embarrassment; it seemed proper that he should talk, and that she should simply look at him. What made it natural was that he was so handsome, or, rather, as she phrased it to herself, so beautiful. The music had been silent for a while, but it suddenly began again; and then he asked her, with a deeper, intenser smile, if she would do him the honour of dancing with him. Even to this inquiry she gave no audible assent; she simply let him put his arm round her waist – as she did so, it occurred to her more vividly than it had ever done before that this was a singular place for a gentleman's arm to be – and in a moment he was guiding her round the room in the harmonious rotation of the polka. When they paused, she felt that she was red; and then, for some moments, she stopped looking at him. She fanned herself, and looked at the flowers that were painted on her fan. He asked her if she would begin again, and she hesitated to answer, still looking at the flowers.

'Does it make you dizzy?' he asked, in a tone of great kindness.

Then Catherine looked up at him; he was certainly beautiful, and not at all red. 'Yes,' she said; she hardly knew why, for dancing had never made her dizzy.

'Ah, well, in that case,' said Mr Townsend, 'we will sit still and talk. I will find a good place to sit.'

He found a good place – a charming place; a little sofa that seemed meant only for two persons. The rooms by this time were very full; the dancers increased in number, and people stood close in front of them, turning their backs, so that Catherine and her companion seemed secluded and unobserved. 'We will talk,' the young man had said; but he still did all the talking. Catherine leaned back in her place, with her eyes fixed upon him, smiling, and thinking him very clever. He had features like young men in pictures; Catherine had never seen such features – so delicate, so chiselled and finished – among the young New Yorkers whom she passed in the streets and met at dancing-parties. He was tall and slim, but he looked extremely strong.

Notes	*agitated:* made nervous	*assent:* saying yes
	acquaintance: a person you know slightly	*singular:* (here) strange
	agreeable: pleasant	*rotation:* turning round
	tongue-tied: unable to think of the right thing to say	*polka:* a lively ballroom dance
	proper: right, correct	*dizzy:* as if everything is spinning
	intenser: stronger, more emotional	*secluded:* out of the way, pleasantly private
	audible: that could be heard	*chiselled:* fine, as if carved

Comprehension

The author

See how much you can remember. Answer these questions quickly, without referring back to page 55.

1 Henry James was educated in ....

2 He did not become a lawyer, but started writing for ....

3 In Paris he met ....

4 He finally decided to settle in ....

5 He wrote over a hundred ....

6 He thought it was more important to concentrate on .... rather than ....

7 Later writers were able to learn from his ....

The text

A Answer these questions.

1 Which of the following means the same as 'consequences' (line 4)?

   a purpose   **b** results   **c** reasons

2 Which of the following means the same as 'embarrassment' (line 5)?

   a shame   **b** dishonour   **c** awkwardness

3 Which of the following means the same as 'particular' (line 10)?

   a private   **b** special   **c** certain

4 Which of the following means the same as 'vividly' (line 18)?

   a strongly   **b** often   **c** brightly

B Answer these questions.

1 Why do you think Catherine is 'always agitated by an introduction' (line 1)?

2 What happens in this conversation when she says nothing?

3 Do you think Mr Townsend is really impressed with the party, the house, the family and Catherine's cousin, or is he just being polite? Do you think he is sincere?

4 Why isn't Catherine embarrassed, although she can't find anything to say?

5 Why does she describe him to herself as beautiful, not handsome?

6 How does she accept his invitation to dance?

7 What happens during the dance?

8 Why do you think she feels dizzy?

9 Why does Catherine like the place he has chosen for them to sit?

10 How much does she contribute to the conversation?

11 How does she feel while he is talking to her?

12 Why is he different from other men she has met?

Discussion

1 Can you explain why Catherine is so attracted to this young man? What impression do you get of him? Do you think he is attracted to her?

2 How do you think this possible romance will turn out? Will they fall in love with each other? Will Catherine's father approve of Mr Townsend? Discuss two or three endings to the story with a partner, and ask the class to choose the best one.

Role-play

Student A: You are Catherine. You are going to explain to your father (Student B) that you have met a wonderful young man, who you would like to marry. Describe all his good qualities to him. You are rather frightened of your father, and very nervous about telling him, but you are also very determined about this.

Student B: You are Dr Sloper. You are horrified to discover that your daughter is considering marrying this man, who you think is simply a fortune-hunter. Try to show her how worthless Mr Townsend is, and remind Catherine how rich she will be one day. But remember that she is old enough to marry without your consent, so you must persuade her rather than threaten her.

Extension

Grammar

'She stopped looking at him' (line 21). Decide whether to use the gerund or the infinitive in the following sentences.

1 Try (turn) the handle the other way. If that doesn't work, we'll have to get a locksmith to come.
2 Stop (talk) and get on with your work!
3 I forgot (lock) the door when I left home this morning.
4 I'm sorry. I meant (send) you a postcard but I forgot your address.
5 I think Fred regrets (leave) school at 16.
6 She's been trying (get) a job, but with no success, I'm afraid.
7 We regret (inform) you that the post you applied for is no longer available.
8 Passing the exam will mean (study) very hard.
9 On the way home he stopped (buy) a bunch of flowers for Janice.

10 I'll never forget (bump) into Michael Jackson in Los Angeles! I got his autograph, of course.

Relative pronouns

'What made it natural was ...' (line 13). Use *what, which* or *that* correctly in the following sentences.

1 .... I like best for lunch is a salad.
2 He spoke very rudely to me, ... upset me.
3 Malaria, ... is carried by mosquitoes, is still a danger for travellers in certain tropical regions.
4 The only car .... he's ever driven was an automatic.
5 I'll take the blue one. It's just .... I want.
6 Terry has two cars, one of .... is a Porsche.
7 Did you hear .... he said?
8 I expect you'll get the job, in .... case I'll resign.
9 They'll have to tell me exactly .... to do.
10 Do you know of anywhere .... won't charge me a fortune to service my car?

Composition (120 – 180 words)

1 Write a letter from Catherine to a close friend of hers, describing the good-looking young man she has just met.
2 Write a composition describing your first meeting with an important person in your life, and explaining why this person is important to you.
3 'All that glitters is not gold.' Are first impressions reliable? Discuss.

14

ROBERT LOUIS STEVENSON

1850 – 1894

Robert Louis Stevenson was born in Edinburgh, Scotland, the son of an engineer. His father wanted him to become an engineer too, but he studied law instead, although he never worked as a lawyer. His health was poor, so he travelled constantly in search of a comfortable climate. He began to write magazine articles and travel books, and in 1880, during a stay in the United States, he married an American woman. In 1889 he settled in Samoa, in the South Seas, and died there of tuberculosis five years later.

Stevenson was an extremely popular writer in the nineteenth century, and managed to produce several completely different styles of work. His *Travels with a Donkey in the Cevennes* is a good example of his travel writing, whereas *The Strange Case of Dr Jekyll and Mr Hyde* is a first-rate thriller. He wrote historical romances, including *Kidnapped*, *The Black Arrow* and *The Master of Ballantrae*, but he is most famous for *Treasure Island*, which marked the start of his popularity. It is a children's classic, but it is much more than just an exciting story, with its recreation of a chilling atmosphere and its powerful portrayal of character.

Well-known works by Robert Louis Stevenson include: *Travels with a Donkey in the Cevennes* (1879), *Treasure Island* (1883), *The Strange Case of Dr Jekyll and Mr Hyde* (1886), *Kidnapped* (1886), *The Black Arrow* (1888), *The Master of Ballantrae* (1889).

Treasure Island

The story is told by Jim Hawkins, a boy whose mother keeps an inn called the 'Admiral Benbow' in the south-west of England. An old pirate captain stays at the inn for some time. He is clearly frightened of a visitor who comes to see him, an evil-looking blind man with a stick. It seems as if the pirate has something that his former shipmates want, locked away in his old wooden sea-chest.

In this extract, the pirate has died, and Jim and his mother decide to open the chest, to look for money he owes them. There is not much time, because they feel sure that the blind man and the rest of the pirates will be back soon.

In the meantime we had found nothing of any value but the silver and the trinkets, and neither of these were in our way. Underneath there was an old boat-cloak, whitened with sea-salt on many a harbour-bar. My mother pulled it up with impatience, and there lay before us, the last things in the chest, a bundle tied up in oilcloth, and looking like papers, and a canvas bag, that gave forth, at a touch, the jingle of gold.

'I'll show these rogues that I'm an honest woman,' said my mother. 'I'll have my dues, and not a farthing over.' • • • And she began to count over the amount of the captain's score from the sailor's bag into the one that I was holding.

It was a long, difficult business, for the coins were of all countries and sizes – doubloons, and louis-d'ors, and guineas, and pieces of eight, and I know not what besides, all shaken together at random. The guineas, too, were about the scarcest, and it was with these only that my mother knew how to make her count.

When we were about half-way through, I suddenly put my hand upon her arm; for I had heard in the silent, frosty air a sound that brought my heart into my mouth – the tap-tapping of the blind man's stick upon the frozen road, it drew nearer and nearer, while we sat holding our breath. Then it struck sharp on the inn-door, and then we could hear the handle being turned, and the bolt rattling as the wretched being tried to enter; and then there was a long time of silence both within and without. At last the tapping recommenced, and, to our indescribable joy and gratitude, died slowly away again until it ceased to be heard.

'Mother,' said I, 'take the whole and let's be going'; for I was sure the bolted door must have seemed suspicious, and would bring the whole hornet's nest about our ears; though how thankful I was that I had bolted it, none could tell who had never met that terrible blind man.

But my mother, frightened as she was, would not consent to take a fraction more than was due to her, and was obstinately unwilling to be content with less. It was not yet seven, she said, by a long way; she knew her rights and she would have them; and she was still arguing with me, when a little low whistle sounded a good way off upon the hill. That was enough, and more than enough, for both of us.

'I'll take what I have,' she said, jumping to her feet.

'And I'll take this to square the count,' said I, picking up the oilskin packet.

Next moment we were both groping downstairs, leaving the candle by the empty chest; and the next we had opened the door and were in full retreat. We had not started a moment too soon. The fog was rapidly dispersing; already the moon shone quite clear on the high ground on either side; and it was only in the exact bottom of the dell and round the tavern door that a thin veil still hung unbroken to conceal the first steps of our escape. Far less than half-way to the hamlet, very little beyond the bottom of the hill, we must come forth into the moonlight. Nor was this all; for the sound of several footsteps running came already to our ears, and as we looked back in their direction, a light tossing to and fro, and still rapidly advancing, showed that one of the newcomers carried a lantern.

Notes	*trinkets:* worthless jewellery

Notes
trinkets: worthless jewellery
were in our way: (archaic) were what we wanted
cloak: a coat with no sleeves
harbour-bar: a sandbank near a harbour
oilcloth: waterproof cloth
canvas: a kind of strong cloth
jingle: the sound of coins
rogues: bad men
a farthing: a quarter of a penny (no longer in use)
the captain's score: what the captain owed
doubloons, louis-d'ors, guineas, pieces of eight: different gold coins

the scarcest: the fewest
bolt: a metal bar to lock a door
wretched being: (here) horrible creature
hornet: a large stinging insect
obstinately: stubbornly, refusing to be persuaded
groping: feeling our way in the dark
dispersing: disappearing
dell: (poetic) a valley
tavern: an inn
a thin veil: a little fog
hamlet: a small village
lantern: a light for use outside

Comprehension

The author

Correct these sentences if necessary. Tick any sentences which are already correct.

1 Stevenson's father wanted him to become an engineer.
2 Stevenson travelled widely on business.
3 He married a Samoan woman.
4 He died in North America.
5 He was not old when he died.
6 He is most famous for his travel writing.

The text

A Match these words or phrases from the text with their meanings.

1	a bundle (line 4)	a	made the sound of
2	gave forth (line 5)	b	began again
3	recommenced (line 19)	c	thankfulness
4	gratitude (line 19)	d	several things tied together
5	consent (line 25)	e	quickly
6	a fraction (line 25)	f	agree
7	conceal (line 36)	g	a tiny part
8	rapidly (line 40)	h	hide

B Rewrite these phrases or sentences in your own words.

1 I'll have my dues, and not a farthing over (line 6).
2 and I know not what besides (line 10)
3 at random (line 11)
4 that brought my heart into my mouth (line 14)
5 within and without (line 18)
6 let's be going (line 21)
7 bring the whole hornet's nest about our ears (line 22)
8 a good way off (line 28)
9 to square the count (line 31)
10 were in full retreat (line 33)

C Answer these questions.

1 What are the various things that Jim and his mother find in the chest?
2 Why doesn't Jim's mother take all the money?
3 Why is it difficult to count the coins?
4 Which coins is Mrs Hawkins most familiar with?
5 What very frightening sound does Jim hear while they are counting?
6 Why is Jim so nervous? What is the 'hornet's nest' he is worried about?
7 What is Mrs Hawkins obstinate about?
8 What finally makes Jim and his mother stop counting and leave?

9 What do they take with them?

10 How does the fog help them to escape?

11 What problems have they got to overcome to reach safety?

12 Who do you think the 'newcomers' are?

Discussion

1 Imagine what might be in the 'bundle tied up in oilcloth ... looking like papers' (line 4). Do you think it will be worth anything?

2 Can you imagine why Jim finds the blind man so frightening? Describe what you think the man might look like.

3 What do you think happens next in the story? Where are Jim and his mother going? Do you think they manage to escape, or are they caught by the 'newcomers'? If they are caught, what will happen to them?

4 Why do you think this book is called *Treasure Island*?

Extension

Word-building

'Whitened with sea-salt' (line 3). Make verbs ending in -*en* from the following adjectives.

1 long
2 straight
3 flat
4 deep
5 loose
6 wide
7 black
8 red
9 strong
10 short
11 dark
12 tight

Expressions

'At a touch' (line 5), 'at random' (line 11). Find expressions using *at* which mean approximately the same as the following.

1 the first time I saw
2 immediately
3 sometimes
4 finally
5 in the night
6 with a quick look
7 the minimum
8 the maximum

Grammar

'To our indescribable joy and gratitude ...' (line 19). Change these sentences so that they start with *To* plus an abstract noun, like the example.

1 I was horrified to see that one of the windows was broken.

2 She was delighted to discover she had passed all her exams.

3 They were very surprised when they sold their house at a profit.

4 We were amazed when we didn't have to pay for the theatre tickets.

5 I was astonished to see that he had aged considerably since our last meeting.

6 How relieved she was when her children returned home safe and sound!

Composition (120 – 180 words)

1 Write the next three paragraphs in the story of *Treasure Island*.

2 Write a description of the 'Admiral Benbow' inn and the surrounding countryside, as you imagine it to be.

3 'Honesty is the best policy.' Do you agree with this saying? Can you think of situations where honesty is *not* the best policy? Write down your opinions.

15

JEROME K. JEROME

1859 – 1927

Jerome Klapka Jerome was born in Walsall in Staffordshire, England, and brought up in east London. His father was an unsuccessful ironmonger. Jerome was at various times a clerk, a schoolmaster, a reporter, an actor and a journalist. He became joint editor of a humorous magazine called *The Idler* in 1892, and then started his own weekly paper called *To-Day*.

Jerome wrote articles, plays and novels, but is best known for his highly amusing *Three Men in a Boat*, which immediately became a humorous classic and has been appreciated as such by several generations of readers. It still maintains its popularity: as the author modestly says, 'The world has been very kind to this book.'

Well-known works by Jerome K. Jerome include: *Three Men in a Boat* (1889), *Idle Thoughts of an Idle Fellow* (1889), *Three Men on the Bummel* (1900), *Paul Kelver* (1902) and the play *The Passing of the Third Floor Back* (1907).

Three Men in a Boat

This book is the account of a boat trip up the River Thames from Kingston to Oxford, and the adventures which the three men (Harris, George and the writer) and the dog (Montmorency) have on the way.

In this extract, they have decided to stop for a picnic lunch. The boat is safely moored, and the three friends are just about to start eating on the river bank.

We were sitting in a meadow, about ten yards from the water's edge, and we had just settled down comfortably to feed. Harris had the beefsteak pie between his knees, and was carving it, and George and I were waiting with our plates ready.

'Have you got a spoon there?' says Harris; 'I want a spoon to help the gravy with.'

The hamper was close behind us, and George and I both turned round to reach one out. We were not five seconds getting it. When we looked round again, Harris and the pie were gone!

It was a wide, open field. There was not a tree or a bit of hedge for hundreds of yards. He could not have tumbled into the river, because we were on the water side of him, and he would have had to climb over us to do it.

George and I gazed all about. Then we gazed at each other.

'Has he been snatched up to heaven?' I queried.

'They'd hardly have taken the pie, too,' said George.

There seemed weight in this objection, and we discarded the heavenly theory.

'I suppose the truth of the matter is,' suggested George, descending to the commonplace and practicable, 'that there has been an earthquake.'

And then he added, with a touch of sadness in his voice: 'I wish he hadn't been carving that pie.'

With a sigh, we turned our eyes once more towards the spot where Harris and the pie had last been seen on earth; and there, as our blood froze in our veins and our hair stood up on end, we saw Harris's head – and nothing but his head – sticking bolt upright among the tall grass, the face very red, and bearing upon it an expression of great indignation!

George was the first to recover.

'Speak!' he cried, 'and tell us whether you are alive or dead – and where is the rest of you?'

'Oh, don't be a stupid ass!' said Harris's head. 'I believe you did it on purpose.'

'Did what?' exclaimed George and I.

'Why, put me to sit here – darn silly trick! Here, catch hold of the pie.'

And out of the middle of the earth, as it seemed to us, rose the pie – very much mixed up and damaged; and after it scrambled Harris – tumbled, grubby and wet.

He had been sitting, without knowing it, on the very verge of a small gully, the long grass hiding it from view; and in leaning a little back he had shot over, pie and all.

He said he had never felt so surprised in all his life, as when he first felt himself going, without being able to conjecture in the slightest what had happened. He thought at first that the end of the world had come.

Notes	*meadow:* a field, usually full of grass
	ten yards: approximately ten metres
	feed: to eat (usually for animals)
	carving: cutting
	gravy: meat sauce
	hamper: a large picnic basket
	tumbled: fallen
	snatched: taken suddenly
	discarded: rejected, threw out
	commonplace: ordinary

practicable: possible
bolt upright: very straight up
indignation: anger
stupid ass: a foolish person
darn: a mild swearword, like 'damn'
scrambled: climbed with difficulty
grubby: dirty
verge: edge
gully: a small ditch or channel
conjecture: to guess, imagine

Comprehension

The author

Complete the sentences in your own words.

1 Jerome K. Jerome was brought up in ....
2 He had many ....
3 He was the editor of ....
4 His best-known work is ....
5 However, he also wrote ....

The text

A Rewrite these phrases or sentences in your own words.

1 We were not five seconds getting it (line 6)
2 There seemed weight in this objection (line 14)
3 we discarded the heavenly theory (line 14)
4 with a touch of sadness in his voice (line 17)
5 as our blood froze in our veins (line 20)
6 he had shot over, pie and all (line 33)

B Answer these questions.

1 What are George and the narrator waiting for?
2 Why do the two men both turn round?
3 Why can't Harris have fallen into the river?
4 Why do George and the narrator decide Harris can't have been taken up to heaven?
5 Who are 'they' in line 13?
6 Why does George speak rather sadly in line 17?

7 Why are the two men so horrified when Harris reappears?
8 Why is Harris so angry?
9 What is the explanation for Harris's sudden disappearance?
10 What is Harris's first thought when he falls backwards?

Discussion

1 What are the only reasons George and the narrator can think of for Harris's disappearance? Why is neither of these at all likely? Why don't they think of the real reason?

2 Does this passage make you laugh? If so, what is funny about it? Find the parts which are most amusing.

Role-play

Students A and B: You are waiting outside the Odeon cinema for your friend (Student C). He/She has not arrived yet and is very late. Try to imagine what might have happened to him/her. When he/she arrives, point out how late he/she is.

Student C: You arrive at the Odeon very late, and very indignant because you are sure your friends arranged to meet you at the Regent, not the Odeon. The reason you're late is because you've been waiting for them at the Regent. Explain that it's all their fault.

Extension

Grammar

A 'He could not have tumbled into the river' (line 9). Complete the following sentences, to show that something could not have happened.

1 She .... (get the job) because she didn't have the right qualifications.
2 He .... (cause the accident) because he was watching television with me all evening.
3 He didn't see her, so he .... (pass on the message).
4 She wasn't in the office that day, so she .... (translate that letter).
5 They .... (see the Queen in London yesterday), because she set off on her round-the-world trip last week.

B 'There has been an earthquake' (line 16). Complete these sentences with the correct form of the present perfect or the past simple.

1 We (buy) all our books yesterday.
2 Oh, no! I (lose) my keys!
3 You ever (win) a prize?
4 I (write) ten letters before lunch yesterday.
5 They first (come) to England in 1988.
6 I (see) several interesting new films lately.
7 It's the first time she (make) a speech in public.
8 They (get) married five years ago.
9 He (not do) much work up to now.
10 The last time I (see) him (be) when he (visit) me in Edinburgh.

C 'In the slightest' (line 35). Make superlatives from these adjectives.

1 comfortable	3 bad	5 far
2 good	4 old	6 light

7 convenient	9 big	11 heavy
8 tired	10 modern	12 gentle

Vocabulary

'George and I gazed all about' (line 11). These words are all ways of looking: *gaze glance glare glimpse peer peep stare*. Use them correctly in the following sentences.

1 Eleanor .... dreamily out of the window.
2 I only caught a .... of the President as his limousine drove by.
3 .... through the mist, we managed to find our way down the mountain.
4 The cyclist picked himself up and .... angrily at the van-driver.
5 Before crossing the road, she .... quickly to her right.
6 The old lady .... inquisitively through her curtains, hoping that nobody would see her.
7 It's rude to .... at people.

Composition (120 – 180 words)

1 Write about a day you spent in the country with some friends. Describe why you decided to go, what your preparations were, and what you did during the day.

2 A student magazine is running a series of articles on planning excursions. You have been asked to write an article on arranging picnics, giving advice on where to go, what kind of food to prepare, and what activities (if any) to organize.

3 Write a composition about the advantages and disadvantages of living in the town or the country.

16

OSCAR WILDE

1854 – 1900

Oscar Wilde was born in Dublin, Ireland. His father was a distinguished doctor, and his mother wrote poetry. He was educated in Ireland, and at Oxford University. He won prizes for his poetry, and set out to shock the respectable middle classes by wearing 'poetic' clothes and long hair. He was well known for his conversation and wit, and had many famous friends among the European artists, painters, actors and writers of the time.

Wilde travelled to North America, where he made a successful lecture tour, and Paris, but eventually returned to England to work first as a journalist, and then as a writer, at which he was very successful. In 1895, however, he was sent to prison for two years for immorality, which ruined his literary career. He died in exile in Paris in 1900.

Wilde's writing was often condemned by his many critics, but his plays were extremely popular, especially *The Importance of Being Earnest,* his most famous work and one of the greatest English comedies. Although his output was uneven, he was among the best writers of his generation, and many quotations from his plays have become household sayings.

Well-known works by Oscar Wilde include: *The Picture of Dorian Gray* (1891), *Lady Windermere's Fan* (1892), *A Woman of No Importance* (1893), *The Importance of Being Earnest* (1895), *An Ideal Husband* (1895), *The Ballad of Reading Gaol* (1898), *De Profundis* (1905).

The Picture of Dorian Gray

This book, his only novel, was written by Oscar Wilde after a dinner with Sir Arthur Conan Doyle, when both writers were asked to write a story for publication in a magazine. Conan Doyle wrote *The Sign of Four,* and Wilde wrote *The Picture of Dorian Gray.* It is a brilliant but rather disturbing story of a young man who sells his soul in order to keep his youth and good looks. As Dorian Gray says when he looks at his portrait, 'If it were I who were to be always young and the picture to grow old ... I would give my soul for it.'

In this extract, the painter and a friend of his, a wealthy lord, are discussing the portrait.

The studio was filled with the rich odour of roses, and when the light summer wind stirred amidst the trees of the garden, there came through the open door the heavy scent of the lilac, or the more delicate perfume of the pink-flowering thorn.

• • • • •

In the centre of the room, clamped to an upright easel, stood the full-length portrait of a young man of extraordinary personal beauty, and in front of it, some little distance away, was sitting the artist himself, Basil Hallward, whose sudden disappearance some years ago caused, at the time, such public excitement, and gave rise to so many strange conjectures.

As the painter looked at the gracious and comely form he had so skilfully mirrored in his art, a smile of pleasure passed across his face, and seemed about to linger there. But he suddenly started up, and, closing his eyes, placed his fingers upon the lids, as though he sought to imprison within his brain some curious dream from which he feared he might awake.

'It is your best work, Basil, the best thing you have ever done,' said Lord Henry, languidly. 'You must certainly send it next year to the Grosvenor. The Academy is too large and too vulgar. Whenever I have gone there, there have been either so many people that I have not been able to see the pictures, which was dreadful, or so many pictures that I have not been able to see the people, which was worse. The Grosvenor is really the only place.'

'I don't think I shall send it anywhere,' he answered, tossing his head back in that odd way that used to make his friends laugh at him at Oxford. 'No: I won't send it anywhere.'

Lord Henry elevated his eyebrows, and looked at him in amazement through the thin blue wreaths of smoke that curled up • • • from his • • • cigarette. 'Not send it anywhere? My dear fellow, why? Have you any reason? What odd chaps you painters are! You do anything in the world to gain a reputation. As soon as you have one, you seem to want to throw it away. It is silly of you, for there is only one thing in the world worse than being talked about, and that is not being talked about. A portrait like this would set you far above all the young men in England, and make the old men quite jealous, if old men are ever capable of any emotion.'

'I know you will laugh at me,' he replied, 'but I really can't exhibit it. I have put too much of myself into it.'

Lord Henry stretched himself out on the divan and laughed.

'Yes, I knew you would; but it is quite true, all the same.'

'Too much of yourself in it! Upon my word, Basil, I didn't know you were so vain.'

Notes	*odour:* smell, scent	*curious:* strange
	lilac: a scented flowering bush	*languidly:* lazily
	thorn: a flowering bush with sharp points growing on the stem	*the Grosvenor:* a famous art gallery at the time
	clamped: held in position	*the Academy:* the Royal Academy in London which shows artists' paintings
	easel: a support for a painting	*vulgar:* common, low-class
	conjectures: guesses, imagining	*tossing:* casually throwing
	comely: pleasing, attractive	*elevated:* raised
	linger: stay	*wreaths:* circles
	started: jumped	*divan:* sofa
	sought: tried	*vain:* too pleased with your own appearance

Comprehension

The author

Decide whether the following sentences are true (**T**) or false (**F**).

1 Oscar Wilde was born in England.
2 His father was a distinguished poet.
3 Oscar Wilde enjoyed shocking people.
4 He was an entertaining companion.
5 His plays were more popular than his stories or poems.
6 He had a long and successful literary career.

The text

A Rewrite these phrases or sentences in your own words.

1 of extraordinary personal beauty (line 5)
2 some little distance away (line 5)
3 gave rise to so many strange conjectures (line 7)
4 What odd chaps you painters are! (line 25)
5 to gain a reputation (line 26)
6 Upon my word, Basil (line 35)

B Answer these questions.

1 What is Basil Hallward looking at?
2 What do we learn about Basil's later life?
3 What is impressive about the painting?
4 What are Basil's two very different reactions to the painting?

5 Why doesn't Lord Henry like the Academy? Does he prefer seeing the pictures or the people at an art gallery?
6 Why is Lord Henry so surprised that Basil does not want to exhibit his picture?
7 What is Basil's reason for not exhibiting his picture?
8 How do you know from the text that Lord Henry is very relaxed? Find examples.
9 'Yes, I knew you would' (line 34). Can you complete the sentence with the correct verb?

Discussion

1 There are several of Oscar Wilde's witty sayings in this text. Look at the sentence beginning 'Whenever I have gone there' (line 16). Do you think Lord Henry really prefers looking at the people rather than the pictures? Or is this just a clever thing to say?
Look at the sentence beginning 'It is silly of you' (line 27). What is worse than being talked about? Do you think that is true? If so, why?
Now look at line 30 'if old men ... emotion.' Can you explain why Lord Henry says this? What impression do you get of Lord Henry after this speech of his?

2 Can you think of any reason why Basil might not want to exhibit this portrait? Could there be any connection between the portrait and his later disappearance?

Role-play

Student A: You are trying to persuade your friend (Student B) that the painting/poem/photo he/she has just shown you is really very good. You think he/she should send it to an exhibition/competition.

Student B: You are very modest about what you have produced, and can't believe it is any good. You didn't spend very long on it, and other people have produced much better ones. Try to find out why your friend admires it so much.

Extension

Vocabulary

A 'Make the old men quite jealous' (line 29). Match these adjectives describing personal characteristics with their meanings.

1	energetic	a	listens to your problems
2	brave	b	enjoys meeting people
3	sympathetic	c	doesn't get tired easily
4	envious	d	has lots of original ideas
5	efficient	e	doesn't mind waiting
6	shy	f	wants what someone else has got
7	sociable	g	doesn't worry about personal danger
8	patient	h	is easily hurt
9	sensitive	i	is nervous about meeting people
10	creative	j	does the job well

B 'The artist himself' (line 6). Complete these sentences with the correct word for the person's job.

Someone who

1 cooks meals in a hotel is a(n) .....
2 sells fruit and vegetables is a(n) .....
3 collects rubbish from people's houses is a(n) .....
4 draws up plans for new buildings is a(n) .....
5 plays a part in a film is a(n) .....
6 checks your eyesight is a(n) .....
7 digs for coal underground is a(n) .....
8 sells clothes in a boutique is a(n) .....
9 writes articles for a newspaper is a(n) .....
10 is elected to Parliament is a(n) .....

Grammar

'A portrait like this would set you ...' (line 28). Make sentences in the second conditional about the following situations. Start each sentence with *If you ...* .

1 You haven't sent this portrait to the Grosvenor yet, so you aren't famous.
2 You are too proud to exhibit the portrait.
3 You aren't famous, and so nobody is talking about you.
4 Nobody is talking about you at the moment, and so you don't get many orders for new paintings.
5 You aren't painting many pictures at present, and so you certainly aren't rich.
6 Because you haven't got much money, you can't lead a very exciting or luxurious life.

Composition (120 – 180 words)

1 Describe a visit you made to a live concert, an art exhibition, or a play or musical at a theatre. Describe the atmosphere, the event, and your reactions to it.

2 Is art important in our lives? Do we need art to survive, or is it just an expensive luxury? Give your opinions.

3 Write a short article for your class magazine, saying whether or not you would recommend your fellow-students to read *The Picture of Dorian Gray*, and giving your reasons.

17

SIR ARTHUR CONAN DOYLE

1859 – 1930

Arthur Conan Doyle was born in Edinburgh, Scotland, the son of a civil servant. He studied medicine and then worked as a doctor for eight years. To add to his income he started writing short stories, which were published in magazines. His first novel *A Study in Scarlet* had as its main character a detective called Sherlock Holmes. This strange intellectual figure, based in his fictional home in London's Baker Street, soon attracted public interest, and Conan Doyle was asked to write Sherlock Holmes stories for publication in the well-known *Strand Magazine*.

Conan Doyle is famous for creating the best-known detective in literature and his good-natured companion Dr Watson. He himself, however, preferred writing his many historical romances, such as *The White Company*. He became bored with his hero Holmes, and tried to kill him off in a story called *The Final Problem*, but the public outcry was so great that Holmes had to be brought back to life in one of his best adventures, *The Hound of the Baskervilles*.

During the Boer War (1899-1902), Conan Doyle worked as a physician at a field hospital in South Africa. In 1902 he received a knighthood for his pamphlet about the war, *The War in South Africa*.

Well-known works by Sir Arthur Conan Doyle include: *A Study in Scarlet* (1887), *The Sign of Four* (1890), *The White Company* (1890), *The Hound of the Baskervilles* (1902), *The Valley of Fear* (1914). The Sherlock Holmes stories are collected in: *The Adventures of Sherlock Holmes* (1892), *The Memoirs of Sherlock Holmes* (1894), *The Return of Sherlock Holmes* (1905) and *The Case Book of Sherlock Holmes* (1927).

The Hound of the Baskervilles

Sherlock Holmes and his friend Dr Watson have been asked to solve the mystery of the death of Sir Charles Baskerville, which was apparently caused by the sudden appearance of a huge and terrifying dog, the ghostly 'hound of the Baskervilles'. Holmes wants to protect young Sir Henry Baskerville from a similar fate, and suspects someone of wanting to murder Sir Henry.

In this extract, Watson describes the scene as he and Holmes are waiting on the moors for Sir Henry to walk past them on his way home. He is alone, and the night is dark and foggy. A perfect opportunity for murder...

The farther wall of the orchard was already invisible, and the trees were standing out of a swirl of white vapour. As we watched it the fog-wreaths came crawling round both corners of the house and rolled slowly into one dense bank, on which the upper floor and the roof floated like a strange ship upon a shadowy sea. Holmes struck his hand

5 passionately upon the rock in front of us, and stamped his feet in his impatience.

'If he isn't out in a quarter of an hour, the path will be covered. In half an hour we won't be able to see our hands in front of us.'

'Shall we move farther back upon higher ground?'

'Yes, I think it would be as well.'

10 So as the fog-bank flowed onwards we fell back before it until we were half a mile from the house, and still that dense white sea, with the moon silvering its upper edge, swept slowly and inexorably on.

'We are going too far,' said Holmes. 'We dare not take the chance of his being overtaken before he can reach us. At all costs we must hold our ground where we are.'

15 He dropped on his knees and clapped his ear to the ground. 'Thank Heaven, I think that I hear him coming.'

A sound of quick steps broke the silence of the moor. Crouching among the stones we stared intently at the silver-tipped bank in front of us. The steps grew louder, and through the fog, as through a curtain, there stepped the man whom we were awaiting.

20 He looked round him in surprise as he emerged into the clear, star-lit night. Then he came swiftly along the path, passed close to where we lay, and went on up the long slope behind us. As he walked he glanced continually over either shoulder, like a man who is ill at ease.

'Hist!' cried Holmes, and I heard the sharp click of a cocking pistol. 'Look out! It's

25 coming!'

There was a thin, crisp, continuous patter from somewhere in the heart of that crawling bank. The cloud was within fifty yards of where we lay, and we glared at it, all three, uncertain what horror was about to break from the heart of it. I was at Holmes's elbow, and I glanced for an instant at his face. It was pale and exultant, his eyes shining

30 brightly in the moonlight. But suddenly they started forward in a rigid, fixed stare, and his lips parted in amazement. At the same instant Lestrade gave a yell of terror and threw himself face downwards upon the ground. I sprang to my feet, my inert hand grasping my pistol, my mind paralysed by the dreadful shape which had sprung out upon us from the shadows of the fog. A hound it was, an enormous coal-black hound,

35 but not such a hound as mortal eyes have ever seen. Fire burst from its open mouth, its eyes glowed with a smouldering glare, its muzzle and hackles and dewlap were outlined in flickering flame. Never in the delirious dream of a disordered brain could anything more savage, more appalling, more hellish be conceived than that dark form and savage face which broke upon us out of the wall of fog.

Notes	*hound:* a kind of dog	*patter:* sound of an animal's feet
	orchard: a large group of fruit trees	*fifty yards:* about fifty metres
	swirl: a round moving shape	*exultant:* joyful, triumphant
	white vapour: mist	*rigid:* stiff, unmoving
	fog-wreaths: circles of fog	*Lestrade:* a police inspector with Holmes and Watson
	inexorably: in a way that cannot be stopped	*inert:* unmoving
	hold our ground: stay	*pistol:* a gun
	moor: open rough land	*muzzle, hackles, dewlap:* all parts of a dog's head, face and neck
	crouching: bending down	*delirious:* feverish
	ill at ease: uncomfortable	*appalling:* terrible
	Hist!: (archaic) Listen!	
	cocking: making a gun ready to fire	

Comprehension

The author

Correct these sentences if necessary. Tick any sentences which are already correct.

1 Sir Arthur Conan Doyle was born in London.
2 He studied medicine for eight years.
3 Sherlock Holmes first appeared in *The Hound of the Baskervilles*.
4 The public preferred Conan Doyle's historical romances.
5 Conan Doyle tried to kill off Sherlock Holmes for ever in *The Final Problem*.
6 He was knighted for his short stories.

The text

A Match these words from the text with their meanings.

1	farther (line 1)	a	looked quickly
2	dense (line 3)	b	thick
3	emerged (line 20)	c	wild
4	swiftly (line 21)	d	human
5	glanced (line 22)	e	came out
6	crisp (line 26)	f	fast
7	continuous (line 26)	g	more distant
8	amazement (line 31)	h	not stopping
9	mortal (line 35)	i	astonishment
10	savage (line 38)	j	hard and dry

B Rewrite these phrases or sentences in your own words.

1 I think it would be as well (line 9)
2 we fell back before it (line 10)
3 At all costs (line 14)
4 clapped his ear to the ground (line 15)
5 from the heart of it (line 28)
6 his lips parted (line 31)
7 gave a yell of terror (line 31)
8 my mind paralysed (line 33)
9 smouldering glare (line 36)
10 a disordered brain (line 37)

C Answer these questions.

1 What makes it difficult for Holmes and Watson to see the path?
2 What is compared to 'a strange ship' (line 4)?
3 What is worrying Holmes?
4 Why do they move away from the house?
5 Who or what are Holmes and Watson waiting for?
6 Who do you think is cocking a pistol (line 24)?
7 Why do you think Holmes is 'exultant' (line 29)?
8 Why does Lestrade throw himself on the ground?
9 Why is Watson's hand 'inert' and his mind 'paralysed'?
10 Describe in your own words the 'hound' that the three men see.

Discussion

1 What gives this story its frightening atmosphere? Do you think the 'hound' is real or a ghost? Can you explain its unusual appearance?

2 Do you feel confident that Holmes can solve the mystery? Why? Can you imagine what steps Holmes will take next?

3 What part does Watson play in the story? Does Holmes really need him? Why do you think Conan Doyle invented Watson? Discuss the author's possible reasons.

Extension

Vocabulary

A 'The sharp click of a cocking pistol' (line 24). These are all onomatopoeic sounds: *buzz crack crash creak rustle snap splash whizz.* Use them in the following sentences, changing the form if necessary.

1 The flies .... around the open dustbin.
2 There was a loud .... as he poured boiling water into the glass.
3 As I tiptoed up to my room, the stairs .... loudly.
4 She .... her fingers and called to her dog.
5 The waiter dropped the breakfast tray with a ....
6 The golf ball .... past my ear.
7 I wish you wouldn't .... your newspaper while I'm trying to listen to the radio.
8 The children enjoyed .... about in the pool.

B Think of three more common adjectives with approximately the same meaning as *dreadful, appalling* and *hellish* (lines 33 and 38).

1 a..............   2 h..............   3 t..............

Now think of three adjectives meaning the opposite.

4 m..............   5 l..............   6 w..............

Grammar

'If he isn't out in a quarter of an hour, the path will be covered' (line 6). Make more first conditional sentences using the following prompts.

1 I / let you know / I / change my mind.
2 Margaret / probably get / job / she / send in / application form.
3 We / have time / we stop / lunch / on the way.
4 I / give you / lift / You / be / in a hurry.
5 You / not be / careful / you / have / accident.
6 I/ can/ repair / my car / I / be able / use it / tomorrow.
7 He / not invite me / party / I / not go.
8 My nephew / buy / mountain bike / he / save up / enough money.
9 You / can / borrow / my computer / yours / break down.
10 Unless you / go now / you / be too late.

Composition (120 – 180 words)

1 Imagine how the story might end, and write three more paragraphs to finish it.

2 Why are detective stories so popular? Is it because they offer an escape from reality, or an imaginary way of dealing with crime? Explain why you like or dislike them.

3 Write a letter to Sir Arthur Conan Doyle, explaining why you like or dislike a Sherlock Holmes story you have read.

18

JOSEPH CONRAD

1857 – 1924

Joseph Conrad was born Jozef Teodor Konrad Korzeniowski, near Berdichev in the Polish Ukraine. At that time the area was held by Tsarist Russia, and Conrad's father was involved in revolutionary politics. He also wrote plays and poetry, and was able to teach his son English and French. The family were sent into exile in Russia for several years, for political reasons, but returned to Poland, where Joseph went to school.

When his father died of tuberculosis, Joseph was looked after by his uncle. As a boy, he was always very keen on reading, especially English adventure stories. He always wanted to go to sea, and he became a sailor in 1874, later visiting England on one of his voyages. In 1886 he became a British citizen, and in 1894, after twenty years at sea, he settled in England, where he became famous as a novelist.

Conrad is considered by many critics to be one of the finest novelists of the late 19th and early 20th century. This is an even more impressive achievement when we remember that he could not speak English perfectly, and had never heard English spoken until he was twenty-one, although his mastery of the written language was complete. The settings and many factual details in his books all come from his real-life experiences. He is noted for his sea-stories, such as *Lord Jim*, his novels of politics and revolution, such as *Nostromo*, and his exotic foreign settings.

Well-known works by Joseph Conrad include: *The Nigger of the Narcissus* (1897), *Lord Jim* (1900), *Heart of Darkness* (1902), *Nostromo* (1904), *The Secret Agent* (1907), *Under Western Eyes* (1911), *Chance* (1914), *Victory* (1915).

Heart of Darkness

The background for this novel was provided by Conrad's voyage up the River Congo in 1890. The narrator, Marlow, who also appears in *Lord Jim*, tells the story. He is sent by a European trading company to command one of their river steamers in Africa. It is a rather dangerous job because in this particular area there is conflict between the white company officials and traders and the natives.

Marlow hears strange stories of a European trader called Kurtz who is in charge of the most distant trading post, and he is keen to meet him. The situation appears even more dangerous as Marlow's ship approaches Kurtz's trading station.

Towards the evening of the second day we judged ourselves about eight miles from Kurtz's station. I wanted to push on; but the manager looked grave, and told me the navigation up there was so dangerous that it would be advisable, the sun being very low already, to wait where we were till next morning. Moreover, he pointed out that if the warning to approach cautiously were to be followed, we must approach in daylight – not at dusk, or in the dark. This was sensible enough. Eight miles meant nearly three hours' steaming for us, and I could also see suspicious ripples at the upper end of the reach. Nevertheless, I was annoyed beyond expression at the delay, and most unreasonably, too, since one night more could not matter much after so many months. As we had plenty of wood, and caution was the word, I brought up in the middle of the stream. The reach was narrow, straight, with high sides like a railway cutting. The dusk came gliding into it long before the sun had set. The current ran smooth and swift, but a dumb immobility sat on the banks. The living trees, lashed together by the creepers and every living bush of the undergrowth, might have been changed into stone, even to the slenderest twig, to the lightest leaf. It was not sleep – it seemed unnatural, like a state of trance. Not the faintest sound of any kind could be heard. You looked on amazed, and began to suspect yourself of being deaf – then the night came suddenly, and struck you blind as well. About three in the morning some large fish leaped, and the loud splash made me jump as though a gun had been fired. When the sun rose there was a white fog, very warm and clammy, and more blinding than the night. It did not shift or drive; it was just there, standing all round you like something solid. At eight or nine, perhaps, it lifted as a shutter lifts. We had a glimpse of the towering multitude of trees, of the immense matted jungle, with the blazing little ball of the sun hanging over it – all perfectly still – and then the white shutter came down again, smoothly, as if sliding in greased grooves. I ordered the chain, which we had begun to heave in, to be paid out again. Before it stopped running with a muffled rattle, a cry, a very loud cry, as of infinite desolation, soared slowly in the opaque air. It ceased.

• • • • •

The sheer unexpectedness of it made my hair stir under my cap. I don't know how it struck the others: to me it seemed as though the mist itself had screamed.

• • • • •

What we could see was just the steamer we were on, her outlines blurred as though she had been on the point of dissolving, and a misty strip of water, perhaps two feet broad, around her – and that was all. The rest of the world was nowhere, as far as our eyes and ears were concerned. Just nowhere. Gone, disappeared; swept off without leaving a whisper or a shadow behind.

Notes

eight miles: about thirteen kilometres
station: a trading post, a few houses with a store
push on: to continue
steaming: travelling on a steam boat
ripples: small waves
reach: an open stretch of river
lashed: tied
creepers: climbing plants
slenderest: thinnest
trance: an unconscious hypnotic state
clammy: humid, damp
shift: to move

shutter: a moveable screen for a window
matted: twisted and stuck together
grooves: long narrow channels, e.g. to hold sliding doors
the chain: the chain holding the anchor, which is let down into the water to keep the boat from moving
heave in: to pull in
paid out: let out
desolation: sadness, loss, despair
opaque: dense, thick with fog
blurred: not clearly visible
two feet: about 60 centimetres

Comprehension

The author

Complete these sentences in your own words.

1 Joseph Conrad was born in 1857 in ....
2 His father was ....
3 The Conrad family were sent ....
4 Joseph's uncle ....
5 Joseph learnt his English through ....
6 Until he was twenty-one, he ....
7 He settled in ....
8 His real-life experiences ....

The text

A Rewrite these words or phrases in your own words.

1 grave (line 2)
2 advisable (line 3)
3 Moreover (line 4)
4 at dusk (line 6)
5 annoyed beyond expression (line 8)
6 caution was the word (line 10)
7 brought up (line 10)
8 a dumb immobility sat on the banks (line 13)
9 immense (line 23)
10 a muffled rattle (line 26)

B Answer these questions

1 Why is Marlow, the narrator, keen to continue the journey?
2 Why does the manager think it would be dangerous to continue immediately?
3 Who do you think gave 'the warning to approach cautiously' (line 5)?
4 What are the possible dangers? What might Marlow be afraid of, when he mentions the 'suspicious ripples'?
5 Why do they need 'plenty of wood'?
6 Where do they decide to spend the night?
7 What is unpleasant about the scenery around them?
8 What is the weather like in the morning?
9 What happens as the anchor chain is being let down into the water?
10 What is so horrifying about the cry they hear?
11 How does the thick fog make the people on the boat feel?

Discussion

1 Marlow is impatient to meet Kurtz because he has heard so much about him, and is very annoyed at having to wait another night before meeting him. Can you think of times when you have had to put off something you were particularly looking forward to? Were there good reasons for the postponement? Discuss your feelings at the time.

2 Have you ever been in a situation where you could not see or hear anything? What sort of dangers would you be afraid of in that situation? What kind of action would you take?

3 How do you know from the text that the situation is dangerous? Find examples to show how the author builds up the atmosphere.

Role-play

Student A: You and your friend (Student B) are planning a two-day camping trip in the mountains this weekend. Unfortunately the weather forecast is very bad. Despite this, you are very keen to go, and are determined to persuade your friend.

Student B: You are a more experienced walker and camper than your friend, and feel it would be silly to ignore the weather forecast. You remind him/her how dangerous it can be in the mountains, and suggest postponing the trip until another weekend.

Extension

Easily confused words

'This was sensible enough' (line 6). Choose the correct word from each pair to complete these sentences.

1 He gets very upset if you criticize him – he's so
....
(sensible/sensitive)
2 Everybody enjoys being with her – she's very
....
(sympathetic/likeable)
3 I hope you're going to take his very useful
....
(advice/advise)
4 I'm .... him at 4 o'clock. He made the appointment yesterday.
(expecting/waiting)

5 I had a wonderful time at the party. It was
.... !
(fun/funny)
6 Nothing I say to him has any ....
(affect/effect)
7 Jane's Chinese vase turned out to be completely
....
(invaluable/worthless)
8 Oh dear! I think I've .... my purse at home!
(forgotten/left)

Grammar

'The loud splash made me jump' (line 18). Use the infinitive with or without *to* to complete these sentences.

1 They allowed him (send) a message.
2 She made him (wear) his suit.
3 He was forced (admit) he was wrong.
4 I think I'll let the children (stay up) late tonight.
5 We were made (finish) our homework in class.
6 I was never allowed (come) home late.
7 Travelling by coach always makes her (feel) ill.
8 The army did not let him (go) on leave.

Vocabulary

'There was a white fog' (line 19). Put these words from the text into new sentences of your own: *daylight dusk current fog jungle shadow*.

Composition (120 – 180 words)

1 Describe a place you have visited, which had its own unique atmosphere. Describe the scenery, the weather, and your reactions to the place.

2 How important is water to us? Explain how we need and use water, and describe some types of employment connected with water.

19

E. M. FORSTER

1879 – 1970

Edward Morgan Forster was born in London. His father was an architect. He was an only child, and his childhood was dominated by the women in his family, his great-aunt, his widowed mother and his aunts. Not until fairly late in life was he able to free himself from their influence. He was very unhappy at Tonbridge, the public school he attended, but when he went to Cambridge University he made friends and enjoyed the stimulating intellectual atmosphere. As he had a private income, he did not need to earn his living, so he travelled in Europe, wrote short stories and novels, and gave private lessons. His novels soon established him as a writer of importance. He visited India and Egypt, but wrote no more novels after *A Passage to India*, his best-known work, although he continued a wide range of literary activities.

Since his death there has been a popular revival of Forster's work. His major novels have all been filmed, and most of them have had considerable box-office success. Part of this success is no doubt due to Forster's nostalgic evocation of a past era, which transfers effectively to the screen. Many critics consider *A Passage to India* his masterpiece, in which he presents the spiritual and emotional tensions of two very different cultures with sympathy and directness.

Well-known works by E. M. Forster include: *Where Angels Fear to Tread* (1905), *The Longest Journey* (1907), *A Room with a View* (1908), *Howard's End* (1910), *A Passage to India* (1924).

Where Angels Fear to Tread

Lilia, an attractive widow, falls in love with a young Italian, Gino, whom she meets while on holiday in Italy with a friend, Caroline. Her first husband's family in England are shocked by her behaviour and try to persuade her not to remarry, but despite this she marries Gino. At first Lilia is delighted with her young husband and life in a small Italian town. Gradually, however, she begins to realize that she has made a mistake and is now trapped. She becomes extremely unhappy.

The stairs up to the attic – the stairs no one ever used – opened out of the living-room, and by unlocking the door at the top one might slip out onto the square terrace above the house, and thus for ten minutes walk in freedom and peace.

The key was in the pocket of Gino's best suit – the English check – which he never wore. The stairs creaked and the keyhole screamed; but Perfetta was growing deaf. The walls were beautiful, but as they faced west they were in shadow. To see the light upon them she must walk round the town a little, till they were caught by the beams of the rising moon. She looked anxiously at the house, and started.

It was easy walking, for a little path ran all outside the ramparts. The few people she met wished her a civil good-night, taking her, in her hatless condition, for a peasant. The walls trended round towards the moon; and presently she came into its light, and saw all the rough towers turn into pillars of silver and black, and the ramparts into cliffs of pearl. She had no great sense of beauty, but she was sentimental, and she began to cry; for here, where a great cypress interrupted the monotony of the girdle of olives, she had sat with Gino one afternoon in March, her head upon his shoulder, while Caroline was looking at the view and sketching. Round the corner was the Siena gate, from which the road to England started, and she could hear the rumble of the diligence which was going down to catch the night train to Empoli. The next moment it was upon her, for the highroad came towards her a little before it began its long zigzag down the hill.

The driver slackened, and called to her to get in. He did not know who she was. He hoped she might be coming to the station.

'Non vengo!' she cried.

He wished her good-night, and turned his horses down the corner. As the diligence came round she saw that it was empty.

'Vengo ...'

Her voice was tremulous, and did not carry. The horses swung off.

'Vengo! Vengo!'

He had begun to sing, and heard nothing. She ran down the road screaming to him to stop – that she was coming; while the distance grew greater and the noise of the diligence increased. The man's back was black and square against the moon, and if he would but turn for an instant she would be saved. She tried to cut off the corner of the zigzag, stumbling over the great clods of earth, large and hard as rocks, which lay between the eternal olives. She was too late; for, just before she regained the road, the thing swept past her, thunderous, ploughing up choking clouds of moonlit dust.

She did not call any more, for she felt very ill, and fainted; and when she revived she was lying in the road, with dust in her eyes, and dust in her mouth, and dust down her ears. There was something very terrible in dust at night-time.

'What shall I do?' she moaned. 'He will be so angry.'

And without further effort she slowly climbed back to captivity, shaking her garments as she went.

> **Notes** *attic:* a room under the roof
> *Perfetta:* the Italian servant and cook
> *beams:* rays of light
> *ramparts:* town walls
> *civil:* polite
> *peasant:* a country person
> *trended:* turned, took her
> *cypress:* a large tree usually found in southern Europe
> *girdle:* a belt or circle
> *sketching:* drawing
>
> *rumble:* a deep noise
> *diligence:* a coach
> *slackened:* reduced speed
> *Non vengo:* (Italian) I'm not coming
> *Vengo:* (Italian) I'm coming
> *tremulous:* nervous, trembling
> *stumbling:* almost tripping
> *clods:* lumps, large pieces
> *garments:* clothes

Comprehension

The author

Complete these sentences in your own words.

1 When E. M. Forster was a child, ...
2 He enjoyed life at university, where he ....
3 He did not get a permanent job because ....
4 The last novel he wrote was called ....
5 People have recently become more aware of his work because ....

The text

A Match these words from the text with their meanings.

1	deaf (line 5)	a	imprisonment
2	anxiously (line 8)	b	soon
3	presently (line 11)	c	columns
4	pillars (line 12)	d	worriedly
5	sentimental (line 13)	e	everlasting
6	eternal (line 34)	f	unable to hear
7	fainted (line 36)	g	emotional
8	captivity (line 40)	h	lost consciousness

B Rewrite these phrases or sentences in your own words.

1 one might slip out (line 2)
2 the keyhole screamed (line 5)
3 taking her ... for a peasant (line 10)
4 a great cypress interrupted the monotony of the girdle of olives (line 14)
5 It was upon her (line 18)
6 Her voice ... did not carry (line 27)
7 if he would but turn for an instant (line 31)
8 without further effort (line 40)

C Answer these questions.

1 Why does Lilia decide to go out?
2 How does she get out of the house?
3 Why doesn't Perfetta hear what is happening?
4 Why does Lilia look 'anxiously' at the house (line 8)?
5 What do the towers and ramparts look like in the moonlight?
6 Why does Lilia begin to cry (line 13)?
7 Where is the coach ('the diligence') going?
8 Why do you think Lilia first shouts '*Non vengo!*' and then '*Vengo!*' to the driver? Why does she change her mind?
9 Why doesn't the driver hear her when she shouts '*Vengo!*'?
10 She thinks 'she would be saved' (line 32). What does she mean?
11 How does she try to stop the coach?
12 What is 'the thing' (line 34)?
13 Why do you think Lilia faints?
14 'He will be so angry' (line 39). Who is 'he' and why will he be so angry?
15 How do you know from the text that Lilia is reluctant to go back to the house?

Discussion

1 Compare the 'freedom and peace' Lilia is looking for in the moonlight with the 'captivity' she has to return to. What do you think her married life is like? Do you think it is a mistake to marry into a different culture?

2 Imagine how the story develops. Will Gino notice she has gone out, and be angry? Will they somehow find a way of living together happily? Or will Lilia manage to get away one day, and return to England?

Extension

Phrasal verbs

'(She) saw all the rough towers turn into pillars of silver and black' (line 12). Complete each sentence with a phrasal verb with *turn*.

1 Can you .... the television if you're not watching it, please?

2 Halfway to the theatre we had to .... because we'd forgotten our tickets.

3 I was .... by the doorman because I wasn't wearing smart enough clothes.

4 Her cousin just .... on her doorstep, out of the blue.

5 The committee .... my offer without even considering it.

6 In the end it .... that an American company had bought the factory.

7 He always .... his family when he needs support.

Conjunctions

Find these conjunctions in the text: *but as till for while before when*. Now use them correctly in the following sentences, using each word only once.

1 .... she wasn't properly qualified, she wasn't offered the job.

2 You can stay with us .... you've found a flat.

3 She told him the truth, ... she had never wanted to deceive him.

4 You've just got time to post that letter .... you do your homework.

5 .... the President came to power, he introduced some important changes in the law.

6 The police car roared past me .... I was walking down the street.

7 They wanted to go on holiday .... they couldn't afford it.

Now use the conjunctions in new sentences of your own.

Relative pronouns

'The stairs no one ever used' (line 1). Turn these pairs of sentences into one sentence and omit the relative pronoun if possible.

1 He gave me the money. I had asked him for it.

2 She resigned her job. I thought that was a mistake.

3 That's the house. Charles Dickens was born there.

4 I ordered the book. You recommended me to read it.

5 He's the official. You spoke to him yesterday.

6 The interviewing panel appointed the applicant. He was the last to be interviewed.

7 I went to collect the post. It was lying on the front doormat.

Composition (120 – 180 words)

Write a story, either beginning *She suddenly realized how she could escape ...*

or ending *There was no escape. She walked slowly back to the house.*

20

D. H. LAWRENCE

1885 – 1930

David Herbert Lawrence was born in Eastwood in Nottinghamshire, England. His father, a coalminer, was comparatively uneducated, but his mother had been a teacher and wanted her children to have a good education. Lawrence won a scholarship to Nottingham High School and did well there. But the family was very poor, so at sixteen he began work as a junior clerk, working long hours and travelling a long way to work each day. He became ill as a result, but was nursed back to health by his mother, who loved him devotedly and possessively.

Lawrence became a teacher, and started writing poetry and a novel. When this first novel, *The White Peacock*, was published, he gave up teaching to write full-time. He travelled widely with his German wife, living in Italy, Australia, the USA and Mexico, and wrote many fine poems, stories, travel books and novels. He died of tuberculosis at the age of 44 near Nice in France.

D. H. Lawrence is one of the best-known literary figures of the twentieth century. His writing often deals with the negative aspects of modern industrial society, contrasted with the beauty of nature and natural feeling. Many people found his books offensive: *Lady Chatterley's Lover* was banned for several years in Britain because of the directness of its language. His novels reflect much of his personal experience, including his uneasy adolescence and his parents' unhappy relationship.

Well-known works by D. H. Lawrence include: *The White Peacock* (1911), *Sons and Lovers* (1913), *The Rainbow* (1915), *Women in Love* (1921), *The Plumed Serpent* (1926), *Lady Chatterley's Lover* (1928).

Sons and Lovers

D. H. Lawrence called *Sons and Lovers* 'an adaptation from life'. The Nottinghamshire coalfields and the conflict in the Morel family are drawn directly from Lawrence's own experience, in this semi-autobiographical novel.

The book was written as a tribute to his mother, whom Lawrence loved and sympathized with. The mother in the story is therefore shown as an intelligent woman. She is more or less resigned to her life with an uncultured working-class husband, a miner, but anxious for her son Paul to fulfil the ambitions which are now unattainable for her. In this passage, however, we see an unusually gentle description of Paul's father, the miner.

He always made his own breakfast. Being a man who rose early and had plenty of time he did not, as some miners do, drag his wife out of bed at six o'clock. At five, sometimes earlier, he woke, got straight out of bed, and went downstairs. When she could not sleep, his wife lay waiting for this time, as for a period of peace. The only real
5   rest seemed to be when he was out of the house.

He went downstairs in his shirt and then struggled into his pit-trousers, which were left on the hearth to warm all night. There was always a fire, because Mrs Morel raked. And the first sound in the house was the bang, bang of the poker against the raker, as Morel smashed the remainder of the coal to make the kettle, which was filled and left
10   on the hob, finally boil. His cup and knife and fork, all he wanted except just the food, was laid ready on the table on a newspaper. Then he got his breakfast, made the tea, packed the bottom of the doors with rugs to shut out the draught, piled a big fire, and sat down to an hour of joy. He toasted his bacon on a fork and caught the drops of fat on his bread; then he put the rasher on his thick slice of bread, and cut off chunks with
15   a clasp-knife, poured his tea into his saucer, and was happy. With his family about, meals were never so pleasant.

He loathed a fork; it is a modern introduction which has still scarcely reached common people. What Morel preferred was a clasp-knife. Then, in solitude, he ate and drank, often sitting, in cold weather, on a little stool with his back to the warm chimney-
20   piece, his food on the fender, his cup on the hearth. And then he read the last night's newspaper – what of it he could – spelling it over laboriously. He preferred to keep the blinds down and the candle lit even when it was daylight; it was the habit of the mine.

At a quarter to six he rose, cut two thick slices of bread-and-butter, and put them in the white calico snap-bag. He filled his tin bottle with tea. Cold tea without milk or
25   sugar was the drink he preferred for the pit. Then he pulled off his shirt, and put on his pit-singlet, a vest of thick flannel cut low round the neck, and with short sleeves like a chemise.

Then he went upstairs to his wife with a cup of tea because she was ill, and because it occurred to him.
30   'I've brought thee a cup o' tea, lass,' he said.

'Well, you needn't, for you know I don't like it,' she replied.

'Drink it up; it'll pop thee off to sleep again.'

She accepted the tea. It pleased him to see her take it and sip it.

'I'll back my life there's no sugar in,' she said.
35   'Yi – there's one big un,' he replied, injured.

'It's a wonder,' she said, sipping again.

Notes	*pit-trousers:* trousers specially for his work as a miner	*loathed:* hated, detested
	hearth: a fireplace	*fender:* a low protective rail around the fireplace
	raked: removed the ashes	*laboriously:* with great difficulty
	poker: a metal rod used to move the coal around in the fire	*calico:* a kind of plain cotton
	kettle: a container for boiling water	*snap-bag:* lunch-bag
	hob: a flat metal surface close to the fire	*thee:* (dialect) you
	rugs: small carpets	*lass:* (dialect) girl
	draught: a current of cold air	*pop:* (colloquial) send
	rasher: a slice of bacon	*back:* bet
	chunks: large pieces	*Yi:* (dialect) yes
	clasp-knife: a folding knife	*big un:* (dialect) big one

Comprehension

The author

Only one ending in each group is correct. Choose the correct one.

1 D. H. Lawrence's parents were
   a both uneducated.
   b both cultured.
   c of different educational backgrounds.
   d both teachers.

2 He became ill because
   a he was forced to work in the mine.
   b he ate badly at home.
   c he had to do two jobs at once.
   d he worked long hours.

3 He gave up teaching
   a when he married.
   b when his first novel was published.
   c to write poetry.
   d when he became ill.

4 His novels show
   a all the details of his parents' life.
   b how unhappy his childhood was.
   c modern industrial society at its best.
   d the conflicts of modern life.

The text

A Rewrite these phrases or sentences in your own words.

1 drag his wife out of bed (line 2)
2 in solitude (line 18)
3 what of it he could (line 21)
4 it was the habit of the mine (line 22)
5 I've brought thee a cup o' tea, lass (line 30)

B Answer these questions.

1 How is Morel different from some miners?
2 What does his wife do while he prepares his breakfast?
3 What is the house like when he has left?
4 Why do you think he gets dressed downstairs?
5 Why does he break up the coal?
6 What does he have for breakfast?
7 Is there a cloth on the table?
8 How does Morel feel about this time, when he is alone by the fire? Why does he feel like this?
9 What does he use instead of a fork?
10 How does he keep warm?
11 What do you know about his education?
12 Why does he like keeping the blinds down and the candle lit?
13 What does he take with him for his lunch?
14 Do you think he always takes his wife a cup of tea?

Discussion

1 How do you think Mrs Morel feels about her husband? And how does Morel feel about her? Do you think it is still a happy marriage? Can you imagine why they might be drifting apart?

2 Are you surprised that Morel is getting his own breakfast? Who does the housework and cooking in your family? Should it be the man, or the woman, or both?

Extension

Grammar

'Well, you needn't ...' (line 31). Make sure you know the difference between *needn't* and *mustn't*. Then put the correct verb in the following sentences.

1 You .... close the windows on your way out. I'll do it myself.
2 He really .... park his car there. It's obstructing the traffic.
3 You .... forget to apply for your visa in time.
4 He .... take any sandwiches because he can have lunch in the factory canteen.
5 You .... buy her any flowers, although I'm sure she'd love some.
6 Tell her she .... wander around that part of town alone at night. It's dangerous.
7 Thank you for offering but, really, you .... come. I'll be quite all right by myself.
8 I'm sorry, you simply .... smoke any more. You'll have to give it up.

Vocabulary

'His thick slice of bread' (line 14). Complete each sentence with one of these words. There is one word more than you need.

slice packet tube carton chunk jar box bar bottle

1 She opened the .... of honey and took out a spoonful.
2 Could I have a .... of plain biscuits, please?
3 Have you got a spare .... of toothpaste?
4 She's just having a .... of yoghurt for lunch.
5 We can light the candles now. Where did I put that .... of matches?
6 He tore a thick .... of bread off the loaf.
7 He occasionally has a .... of chocolate with his coffee in the evening.
8 That cake looks delicious. I think I'll have a ....

Confusing verbs

'At a quarter to six he rose' (line 23). Complete these sentences with the correct form of *rise* or *raise*.

1 The child .... her hand and answered the teacher's question.
2 Prices have .... steeply again this year.
3 The manager .... from his desk and shook hands with me.
4 We'll have to .... his salary if we want to keep him in the job.
5 She .... her eyebrows in surprise.
6 If you get up early enough, you can watch the sun .... over the horizon.

Composition (120 – 180 words)

Describe part of the daily routine of someone you know well, using the past tense, as D. H. Lawrence does. Make sure the reader finds out what connection the person has with you, and what kind of person is being described. Start with *It was always the same. First he/she used to ...*

21

ERNEST HEMINGWAY

1899 – 1961

Ernest Hemingway was born in Chicago, Illinois, USA, the son of a doctor. He worked as a newspaper reporter in Kansas City, then served in World War I as a volunteer with an ambulance unit on the Italian front, where he was badly wounded. After the war he became a reporter for a Canadian newspaper, then married in 1921 and settled in Paris, where there were many American writers and artists. He made his name with his poems, short stories and novels. During this period his writing shows the post-war generation's strong feeling of disillusionment.

Gradually Hemingway began to feel more at home in the world of blood sports, such as bullfighting and big-game hunting, than in literary circles. He actively supported the Republicans in the Spanish Civil War, and was a war correspondent in Europe during World War II. In his later years he lived mostly in Cuba, where he enjoyed deep-sea fishing. He shot himself in 1961, having been depressed and ill for some time.

Some critics consider Hemingway's short stories to be his finest work, but he is best known for his novels *A Farewell to Arms* and *For Whom the Bell Tolls*, which deal with the great themes of love, war, freedom and death. His writing style is plain and simple, as a result of the rules he had learnt as a reporter, and has greatly influenced later writers. He won the Nobel Prize for Literature in 1954.

Well-known works by Ernest Hemingway include: *The Sun Also Rises* (1926), *A Farewell to Arms* (1929), *Death in the Afternoon* (1932), *For Whom the Bell Tolls* (1940), *Across the River and into the Trees* (1950), *The Old Man and the Sea* (1952).

A Farewell to Arms

This novel established Hemingway as one of the most important writers of the 20th century. Set in World I, it is the story of Frederic Henry, an American lieutenant attached to an Italian ambulance unit as a volunteer. Henry falls in love with an English nurse, Catherine Barkley. During the Italian retreat he deserts from the army and escapes with Catherine by boat to Switzerland (a neutral and therefore safe country). Here they stay in a small guest-house in the mountains, where at last they can spend some time together, well away from the fighting.

That fall the snow came very late. We lived in a brown wooden house in the pine trees on the side of the mountain and at night there was frost so that there was thin ice over the water in the two pitchers on the dresser in the morning. Mrs Guttingen came into the room early in the morning to shut the windows and started a fire in the tall porcelain stove. The pine wood crackled and sparkled and then the fire roared in the stove and the second time Mrs Guttingen came into the room she brought big chunks of wood for the fire and a pitcher of hot water. When the room was warm she brought in breakfast. Sitting up in bed eating breakfast we could see the lake and the mountains across the lake on the French side. There was snow on the tops of the mountains and the lake was a grey steel-blue.

Outside, in front of the chalet a road went up the mountain.

· · · · ·

Sometimes we went off the road and on a path through the pine forest. The floor of the forest was soft to walk on; the frost did not harden it as it did the road. But we did not mind the hardness of the road because we had nails in the soles and heels of our boots and the heel nails bit on the frozen ruts and with nailed boots it was good walking on the road and invigorating. But it was lovely walking in the woods.

In front of the house where we lived the mountain went down steeply to the little plain along the lake and we sat on the porch of the house in the sun and saw the winding of the road down the mountain-side and the terraced vineyards on the side of the lower mountain, the vines all dead now for the winter and the fields divided by stone walls, and below the vineyards the houses of the town on the narrow plain along the lake shore. There was an island with two trees on the lake and the trees looked like the double sails of a fishing-boat. The mountains were sharp and steep on the other side of the lake and down at the end of the lake was the plain of the Rhone Valley flat between the two ranges of mountains; and up the valley where the mountains cut it off was the Dent du Midi. It was a high snowy mountain and it dominated the valley but it was so far away that it did not make a shadow.

When the sun was bright we ate lunch on the porch but the rest of the time we ate upstairs in a small room with plain wooden walls and a big stove in the corner. We bought books and magazines in the town and a copy of *Hoyle* and learned many two-handed card games. The small room with the stove was our living-room. There were two comfortable chairs and a table for books and magazines and we played cards on the dining-table when it was cleared away. Mr and Mrs Guttingen lived downstairs and we would hear them talking sometimes in the evening and they were very happy together too. He had been a head waiter and she had worked as maid in the same hotel and they had saved their money to buy this place. They had a son who was studying to be a head waiter. He was at a hotel in Zurich.

Notes *fall:* (American) autumn
pitchers: jugs
dresser: a chest of drawers
crackled: made a noise
the lake: Lake Geneva
chalet: a house in the mountains
nails: metal points in boots to grip the ground more firmly

ruts: deep tracks made by carts
invigorating: making you feel stronger
porch: a covered area outside the door of a house
terraced vineyards: vines growing on several levels
Dent du Midi: a high mountain in the Alps
Hoyle: a well-known book of rules for card games
two-handed: for two people to play

Comprehension

The author

See how much you can remember. Answer the questions quickly without referring back to page 87.

1 In which war was Hemingway a volunteer?
2 Was he American or Canadian?
3 Which side did he support in the Spanish Civil War?
4 When did he win the Nobel Prize for Literature?
5 What was his great interest in later life?
6 How did he die?

The text

A Match these adjectives and nouns to make pairs of words from the text.

1 stone   a lake
2 porcelain   b boots
3 steep   c walls
4 nailed   d vineyards
5 terraced   e stove
6 narrow   f house
7 grey steel-blue g plain
8 wooden   h mountains

B Answer these questions.

1 Why is there thin ice on the water in the jugs every morning?
2 Who is Mrs Guttingen, and why does she come in in the morning?

3 Where do the couple eat breakfast?
4 Why do they wear nailed boots for walking?
5 What can they see on the lake?
6 What is there at the end of the lake?
7 What does 'it' refer to in line 26? Why does it 'dominate the valley'?
8 Where do they eat if it is not sunny?
9 How do they spend their time?
10 Are they happy? Where does the text tell us that?

C Complete these sentences in your own words.

1 Mrs Guttingen came in three times in the morning, first to ...., next to ...., and then to ....
2 From the chalet, you could walk either ...., or ...., or ....
3 Further up the valley there was the Dent du Midi, which ....
4 Sometimes it was sunny enough for the young couple to .... , but most of the time they ate ....
5 Mr and Mrs Guttingen's son did not ....

Discussion

1 Catherine and Frederic lead a very quiet life. Why do you think they appear to be so happy? Would you be happy in this situation, or would you like to meet more people? Discuss what you would like to do if you spent several weeks away from home in a small place in winter.

2 What are the advantages and disadvantages of being in the mountains in winter? If you had a winter holiday, would you prefer to go to a country with a hot climate where you could spend time on the beach?

3 Do you think this happy period will continue? Imagine how the story will develop. Will Catherine and Frederic be able to live happily together in England or America when the war is over?

4 Can you explain Hemingway's title *A Farewell to Arms*? From what you know of his life, why do you think he wrote this novel?

Extension

Grammar

'Sitting up in bed eating breakfast we could see ...' (line 8). Make sentences beginning with a present participle, based on the following sentences.

1 When I came into the room unexpectedly, I found Tim reading my letter.

2 She arrived late for work and discovered the boss waiting by her desk.

3 Because he felt exhausted after his long day, he decided not to cook a meal.

4 As I didn't understand his question, I couldn't give him an answer.

5 She didn't know what else to do, so she rang the police for help.

Vocabulary

A 'He had been a head waiter ... ' (line 35). Complete these sentences with the correct word for someone who works in a hotel.

1 When I returned to my room, the .... hadn't finished making my bed.

2 I asked the .... to carry my cases down to reception for me.

3 The .... apologized for serving my meal so late.

4 There are lots of Italian specialities on the menu, because the hotel has recently taken on an Italian ....

5 If anything is wrong, I always insist on making my complaint to the .... in person.

6 The .... usually asks you to sign the register before giving you your room key.

B 'The pine wood crackled' (line 5). These are some more onomatopoeic verbs: *bang crunch roar whistle snap hiss crash*. Put them correctly into the following sentences.

1 The motorbike .... off down the road.

2 The snake looked dangerous as it lifted its head and .... at me.

3 Roger .... happily as he walked out of the house.

4 'Don't do that!' she .... crossly. 'I've told you before!'

5 The frozen snow .... under our feet as we walked along.

6 He .... the door behind him as he stormed out of the room.

7 The pile of plates suddenly slipped and .... to the floor.

Composition (120 – 180 words)

1 Write a description of a house you know very well. Say why you are familiar with it, and how you feel about it.

2 Write a description of your dream house.

22

GEORGE ORWELL

1903 – 1950

George Orwell is the pen-name of Eric Blair, who was born in Bengal, India, the son of a British civil servant. He won a scholarship to Eton, a famous English public school, where he was very aware of his fellow-pupils' wealthy backgrounds. He joined the Indian Imperial Police in Burma in 1922, but decided he could not support colonialism, and returned to Europe in 1927, determined to make writing his career. First he tried to make a living in Paris, but was so poor he almost starved to death, and had to return to England. He worked at whatever job he could find, and spent his time in the company of other homeless people. The result of this experience was the autobiographical *Down and Out in Paris and London*, a realistic portrayal of poverty. Now he was able to produce several books which brought in enough to live on.

In 1936 Orwell went to fight on the side of the Republicans in the Spanish Civil War. He was wounded and returned to England, where he contributed to literary magazines and daily newspapers as well as publishing essays and novels. He married twice, and died of tuberculosis in 1950.

Orwell communicates his (often political) points very effectively in a plain, colloquial style, which makes his writing very accessible. When *Animal Farm*, a horrifying satire on the Russian Revolution, was published in 1945, he became world famous, and in *Nineteen Eighty-Four* he shows his pessimism about politics, government and the future. These two political satires are still his most popular works.

Well-known works by George Orwell include: *Down and Out in Paris and London* (1933), *The Road to Wigan Pier* (1937), *Homage to Catalonia* (1938), *Animal Farm* (1945), *Nineteen Eighty-Four* (1949).

Down and Out in Paris and London

In this book Orwell describes his real experiences in the severe economic slump of the twenties and thirties. Sometimes he manages to find casual work, which is always hard and badly paid. However, at this point in the book, he has taken to the life of a tramp, and describes one of the tramps he meets on the road.

Paddy was my mate for about the next fortnight, and, as he was the first tramp I had known at all well, I want to give an account of him. I believe that he was a typical tramp and there are tens of thousands in England like him.

He was a tallish man aged about thirty-five, with fair hair going grizzled and watery blue eyes. His features were good, but his cheeks had lanked and had that greyish, dirty-in-the-grain look that comes of a bread and margarine diet. He was dressed, rather better than most tramps, in a tweed shooting-jacket and a pair of very old evening trousers with the braid still on them. Evidently the braid figured in his mind as a lingering scrap of respectability, and he took care to sew it on again when it came loose. He was careful of his appearance altogether, and carried a razor and bootbrush that he would not sell, though he had sold his 'papers' and even his pocket-knife long since. Nevertheless, one would have known him for a tramp a hundred yards away. There was something in his drifting style of walk, and the way he had of hunching his shoulders forward, essentially abject. Seeing him walk, you felt instinctively that he would sooner take a blow than give one.

He had been brought up in Ireland, served two years in the war, and then worked in a metal polish factory, where he had lost his job two years earlier. He was horribly ashamed of being a tramp, but he had picked up all a tramp's ways. He browsed the pavements unceasingly, never missing a cigarette-end, or even an empty cigarette packet, as he used the tissue paper for rolling cigarettes. On our way into Edbury he saw a newspaper parcel on the pavement, pounced on it, and found that it contained two mutton sandwiches, rather frayed at the edges; these he insisted on my sharing. He never passed an automatic machine without giving a tug at the handle, for he said that sometimes they are out of order and will eject pennies if you tug at them. He had no stomach for crime, however. When we were in the outskirts of Romton, Paddy noticed a bottle of milk on a doorstep, evidently left there by mistake. He stopped, eyeing the bottle hungrily.

• • • • •

'Somebody could knock dat bottle off, eh? Knock it off easy.'

I saw that he was thinking of 'knocking it off' himself. He looked up and down the street; it was a quiet residential street and there was nobody in sight. Paddy's sickly, chap-fallen face yearned over the milk. Then he turned away, saying gloomily:

'Best leave it. It don't do a man no good to steal. T'ank God, I ain't never stolen nothin' yet.'

N o t e s	

mate: a friend and companion
tramp: a homeless person who walks from one place to another
grizzled: grey
lanked: become thinner
dirty-in-the-grain: permanently dirty
braid: a sort of narrow ribbon
scrap: a small piece
a hundred yards: about a hundred metres
drifting: aimless, without purpose
hunching: rounding
abject: hopeless, without pride
blow: a punch, a hit
browsed: searched

rolling cigarettes: making his own cigarettes
pounced on it: picked it up quickly
frayed: broken
tug: a pull
eject: to push out
dat: (dialect) that
knock it off: (slang) steal it
sickly: ill-looking
chapfallen: depressed, down-hearted
yearned over: longed for, wanted
It don't do ... no good: (ungrammatical) It doesn't do ... any good
I ain't never stolen nothin': (ungrammatical) I've never stolen anything

Comprehension

The author

See how much you can remember. Answer the questions quickly, without referring back to page 91.

1 Where was Orwell born?
2 Why did he return to Europe in 1927?
3 Why didn't he stay in Paris?
4 Which war did he fight in?
5 Which book made him world famous?
6 How did he feel about the future?

The text

A Rewrite these phrases or sentences in your own words.

1 Down and out
2 I want to give an account of him (line 2)
3 a lingering scrap of respectability (line 9)
4 he would sooner take a blow than give one (line 15)
5 (he had) served two years in the war (line 16)
6 he had picked up all a tramp's ways (line 18)
7 these he insisted on my sharing (line 22)
8 He had no stomach for crime (line 24)
9 Somebody could knock dat bottle off, eh? (28)
10 Best leave it (line 32)

B Answer these questions.

1 Describe Paddy's appearance as well as you can, using adjectives and expressions from the text.
2 Why does he look rather unhealthy, according to the author?
3 Why do you think he always carries a razor and a bootbrush?
4 What do you think 'the papers' he sold were (line 11)?
5 How is he easily recognizable as a tramp?
6 Why did he become a tramp?
7 Describe some of a tramp's habits.
8 Why doesn't Paddy steal the bottle of milk?

Discussion

1 What do you know about Paddy's character from the text? Do you think he will ever find another job, or will he remain a tramp? Is he happy as he is, or not? How would you feel in his situation?

2 There are increasing numbers of homeless people, especially in large cities. Can you suggest any ways of helping them to find jobs and accommodation? If you see a beggar in the street, do you give him/her any money? Why, or why not?

Role-play

Student A: You and your friend Student B have just found a £50 note on the pavement. You think you and your friend should keep it and spend it, as you're rather short of money. Try to make your friend agree with you.

Student B: You aren't sure, but you think you saw a woman drop the note from her bag when she got out of her car and went into a house nearby. You think it's dishonest to keep the money, because it isn't yours. Try to persuade Student A that you should knock on the woman's door and ask her if she's lost £50, or suggest alternative action to take.

Extension

Grammar

'It don't do a man no good ...' (line 32). Put the following ungrammatical sentences into correct English.

1 I never saw nobody.
2 She don't really love him, do she?
3 I ain't gonna tell the truth.
4 They was my friends, all of 'em.
5 He never done it.
6 She don't come here no more.
7 He ain't leaving, not no way.
8 You been there before?

Expressions

'Sometimes they are out of order' (line 24). Complete the following sentences with the correct expression using *out of* and *date breath stock print sight reach pocket control.*

1 He ran up five flights of stairs and arrived completely ....
2 I went on waving at the ship until it was ....

3 The jar is on top of the cupboard, where I can't get it. It's just ....
4 I'm afraid those statistics are rather .... We need more recent information.
5 I spent my own money on the project, so now I'm ....
6 Despite the firemen's efforts, the fire rapidly got .... and raged furiously for several days.
7 I'm sorry, madam, but the size you want is .... at the moment. We could order it for you, if you like.
8 I'm afraid that book's .... now, so you'll just have to try and find a second-hand copy.

Vocabulary

'He was horribly ashamed of being a tramp' (line 17). The following adjectives are all used to describe feelings or personality: *embarrassed generous honest proud reliable selfish.* Use them to complete these sentences.

1 It's very .... of you to tell the truth.
2 Ladies and gentlemen, I must thank you for this extraordinarily .... gift.
3 I'm afraid Sandra is terribly .... She never considers other people.
4 She was very .... when she realized what a silly mistake she had made.
5 I'm sorry to say that Tony is not very .... He may turn up, or he may not.
6 Mr Dickinson is extremely .... of his son's academic achievements.

Composition (120 – 180 words)

Write a description of an interesting person you have met. Make sure you describe his/her character as well as appearance.

23

DAPHNE DU MAURIER

1907 – 1989

Daphne du Maurier was born in London. Her father, a famous actor manager, adored his three daughters but treated them like boys, teaching them to play cricket and taking them to sports matches. He hoped that Daphne would follow in the footsteps of his own father, George du Maurier, who was a well-known writer and illustrator. In fact, she has become much better known than her father or grandfather. Her favourite childhood books were the classic boys' adventure stories by R. M. Ballantyne and Captain Marryat. Throughout her life she wrote a number of successful period romances and adventure stories, as well as novels, thrillers, short stories and plays, many of which have been filmed. She spent as much time as she could in her beloved Cornwall.

Most of Daphne du Maurier's work contains elements of the male adventure story and the female romance. She clearly enjoyed writing as a male narrator (in *My Cousin Rachel*, for instance), but she also identified with her heroines. *Jamaica Inn* was her first best seller, a novel about smuggling and shipwreck, set in Cornwall, in which the heroine never really finds happiness. The author admitted that in *Rebecca* she saw herself partly as the shy, quiet girl who becomes the second Mrs de Winter, and partly as the wild, beautiful Rebecca, Maxim de Winter's first wife.

Well-known works by Daphne du Maurier include: *Jamaica Inn* (1936), *Rebecca* (1938), *Frenchman's Creek* (1942), *My Cousin Rachel* (1951), *The Flight of the Falcon* (1965).

Rebecca

A penniless young girl is working on the French Riviera as a companion to a rich American lady, Mrs Van Hopper, when she meets the handsome and fascinating Maxim de Winter. She knows that he is very wealthy and owns a beautiful country house in England, called Manderley. He appears very attracted to her, despite her lack of self-confidence, and in this extract he seems to be making a proposal. But is he offering her a job, or marriage?

'So that's settled, isn't it?' he said, going on with his toast and marmalade; 'instead of being companion to Mrs Van Hopper you become mine, and your duties will be almost exactly the same. I also like new library books, and flowers in the drawing-room, and bezique after dinner. And someone to pour out my tea. The only difference is that I don't take Taxol, I prefer Eno's, and you must never let me run out of my particular brand of toothpaste.'

I drummed with my fingers on the table, uncertain of myself and of him. Was he still laughing at me, was it all a joke? He looked up, and saw the anxiety on my face. 'I'm being rather a brute to you, aren't I?' he said; 'this isn't your idea of a proposal. We ought to be in a conservatory, you in a white frock with a rose in your hand, and a violin playing a waltz in the distance. And I should make violent love to you behind a palm tree. You would feel then you were getting your money's worth. Poor darling, what a shame. Never mind, I'll take you to Venice for our honeymoon and we'll hold hands in the gondola. But we won't stay too long, because I want to show you Manderley.'

He wanted to show me Manderley... And suddenly I realized that it would all happen; I would be his wife, we would walk in the garden together, we would stroll down that path in the valley to the shingle beach. I knew how I would stand on the steps after breakfast, looking at the day, throwing crumbs to the birds, and later wander out in a shady hat with long scissors in my hand, and cut flowers for the house. I knew now why I had bought that picture postcard as a child; it was a premonition, a blank step into the future.

He wanted to show me Manderley... My mind ran riot then, figures came before me and picture after picture – and all the while he ate his tangerine, giving me a piece now and then, and watching me. We would be in a crowd of people, and he would say, 'I don't think you have met my wife.' Mrs de Winter. I would be Mrs de Winter. I considered my name, and the signature on cheques, to tradesmen, and in letters asking people to dinner. I heard myself talking on the telephone: 'Why not come down to Manderley next weekend?' People, always a throng of people. 'Oh, but she's simply charming, you must meet her –' This about me, a whisper on the fringe of a crowd, and I would turn away, pretending I had not heard.

• • • • •

I saw the polished table in the dining-room, and the long candles. Maxim sitting at the end. A party of twenty-four. I had a flower in my hair. Everyone looked towards me, holding up his glass. 'We must drink the health of the bride,' and Maxim saying afterwards, 'I have never seen you look so lovely.' Great cool rooms, filled with flowers. My bedroom, with a fire in the winter, someone knocking at the door. And a woman comes in, smiling; she is Maxim's sister, and she is saying, 'It's really wonderful how happy you have made him; everyone is so pleased, you are such a success.' Mrs de Winter. I would be Mrs de Winter.

'The rest of the tangerine is sour, I shouldn't eat it,' he said, and I stared at him, the words going slowly to my head, then looked down at the fruit on my plate.

> **N o t e s** *drawing-room:* (old-fashioned) living-room
> *bezique:* a card game for two or more players
> *Taxol, Eno's:* medicines taken for indigestion
> *brute:* a beast
> *proposal:* an offer of marriage
> *conservatory:* a garden room
> *frock:* a dress
> *waltz:* a ballroom dance in triple time
> *make violent love to you:* (old-fashioned usage) pour out my feelings for you
>
> *gondola:* a boat used on canals in Venice
> *shingle:* small stones
> *premonition:* a warning in the mind, of a future event
> *tangerine:* a type of orange
> *tradesman:* a person who comes to someone's house to deliver goods
> *sour:* bitter, bad-tasting

Comprehension

The author

Complete these sentences in your own words.

1 Daphne du Maurier's father taught ....
2 Her favourite reading when she was a child ....
3 Her grandfather ....
4 She wrote many different ....
5 The place she loved most ....

The text

A Rewrite these phrases or sentences in your own words.

1 I'm being rather a brute to you (line 8)
2 You would feel then you were getting your money's worth (line 12)
3 what a shame (line 13)
4 looking at the day (line 19)
5 My mind ran riot then (line 23)
6 always a throng of people (line 29)
7 on the fringe of a crowd (line 30)
8 you are such a success (line 38)

B Find two sentences that

1 outline Maxim's likes and dislikes.
2 show Maxim realizes that she would like a different kind of proposal.
3 indicate what Maxim's immediate plans for the future are.

4 show the narrator is beginning to imagine herself as Mrs de Winter.
5 describe her day-dream of herself as a successful hostess.

C Answer these questions.

1 What is strange about Maxim's proposal?
2 When does the narrator realize the proposal isn't just a joke, and that he is really offering to marry her?
3 Why does she mention a picture postcard? Can you explain its significance?
4 What is Maxim doing while she is day-dreaming about her future life?
5 What is wrong with the tangerine, and what is Maxim's advice about it?

Discussion

1 From your reading of the text, try to describe the narrator's character. Compare her with Maxim. Are they similar or very different? Do you think they will be happy together if they marry? Do you think they love each other?

2 If she becomes his wife, will she be as much of a success as she hopes? Maxim is much older than her, and perhaps has fixed ideas and habits. Imagine what problems she will have to face as the mistress of a great country house. Would you like to be in her shoes?

3 'The rest of the tangerine is sour ...' (line 40). Could this sourness be symbolic? Do you think the author is giving us a clue here, about the development of the story?

4 Do you sometimes day-dream? When? What kinds of day-dream do you have?

Extension

Grammar

A 'So that's settled, isn't it?' (line 1). Put the correct question tags at the end of these sentences.

1 She doesn't like tea, ...?
2 You'd better not go home, ...?
3 She hadn't seen him before, ...?
4 I think they'd rather have a holiday, ...?
5 Let's have lunch now, ...?
6 Get me a sandwich, ...?
7 He had to work overtime, ...?
8 I'm right, ...?
9 We won't be invited, ...?
10 I don't think she's ever written to him, ...?

B 'I also like new library books' (line 3). Decide whether to use the present simple or continuous in the following sentences.

1 I usually (live) in New York, but at the moment I (live) in Venice.
2 He (study) engineering at university at present.
3 Every year they (visit) their grandparents in Italy.
4 Quiet! I (try) to watch the film!
5 She often (have) difficulty finishing her homework.
6 Your theory (appear) to be correct.

7 He usually (eat) fresh fruit and toast for breakfast.
8 You know, this cake (taste) simply delicious.
9 Yes, I can see him now. He just (park) his car outside.
10 Paul (hate) having to wait for people.

Expressions

'Going on with his toast and marmalade' (line 1). We do not say 'marmalade and toast'. The following pairs of words can be linked with *and* to make common phrases. Decide which way round they are used.

1 fish/chips
2 gentlemen/ladies
3 downstairs/upstairs
4 black/white
5 to/fro
6 bread/butter
7 out/in
8 men/women
9 breakfast/bed
10 forwards/backwards

Vocabulary

Put these words from the text into new sentences of your own: *duties brand anxiety proposal honeymoon signature sour pale.*

Composition (120 – 180 words)

1 Write a letter to Mrs Van Hopper, explaining that you have decided to marry Maxim de Winter and that you will therefore no longer be able to act as her companion. The letter should be formal and very polite.

2 Your college magazine has asked you to write about an interesting literary character. Write a short article for the magazine about Maxim de Winter or the narrator, giving details of his/her character, and saying why you find him/her interesting.

24

EVELYN WAUGH

1903 – 1966

Evelyn Waugh was born in Hampstead, London, the son of a publisher. He went to public school and Oxford University, but was more interested in social than academic life. He taught at various schools but did not enjoy teaching. However, his first novel, *Decline and Fall*, which reflected some of his teaching experience, was hugely successful. Waugh travelled widely, and married in 1928. In 1930 he divorced his wife and joined the Roman Catholic Church. He became a well-known novelist, as well as a journalist and travel writer. After marrying again, he settled in the south-west of England.

Waugh is famous for his early novels, works of high comedy which satirize the frivolity of post-war upper-class society. His later novels deal with themes of innocence and guilt, morality and lack of morals. He also wrote a trilogy of World War II novels.

Well-known works by Evelyn Waugh include: *Decline and Fall* (1928), *Vile Bodies* (1930), *A Handful of Dust* (1934), *Brideshead Revisited* (1945), *The Loved One* (1948), *Men at Arms* (1952), *Unconditional Surrender* (1961).

Brideshead Revisited

During World War II Charles Ryder and his men are billeted at Brideshead, which he recognizes as the beautiful mansion belonging to an aristocratic Roman Catholic family he used to know very well. The book continues with Charles's narration of his emotional involvement with this family and the events of his past.

In this extract, Charles is spending the summer at Brideshead with his friend, Sebastian, the younger son, whom he met at university in Oxford. Although Sebastian seems strangely reluctant to have anything to do with his own family, Charles has met Sebastian's elder brother, the Earl of Brideshead, and his sisters, Julia and Cordelia. Charles realizes how important their religion is to all of them, and begins to feel an undercurrent of tension in the family. Sebastian's mother, Lady Marchmain, is very religious and refuses to divorce her husband, Lord Marchmain, who has lived for years in Venice with another woman.

That night I began to realize how little I really knew of Sebastian, and to understand why he had always sought to keep me apart from the rest of his life. He was like a friend made on board ship, on the high seas; now we had come to his home port.

Brideshead and Cordelia went away; the tents were struck on the show ground, the flags uprooted; the trampled grass began to regain its colour; the month that had started in leisurely fashion came swiftly to its end. Sebastian walked without a stick now and had forgotten his injury.

'I think you'd better come with me to Venice,' he said.

'No money.'

'I thought of that. We live on papa when we get there. The lawyers pay my fare – first class and sleeper. We can both travel third for that.'

And so we went; first by the long, cheap sea-crossing to Dunkirk, sitting all night on deck under a clear sky, watching the grey dawn break over the sand dunes; then to Paris, on wooden seats, where we drove to the Lotti, had baths and shaved, lunched at Foyot's, which was hot and half-empty, loitered sleepily among the shops, and sat long in a café waiting till the time of our train; then in the warm, dusty evening to the Gare de Lyon, to the slow train south, again the wooden seats, a carriage full of the poor, visiting their families – travelling, as the poor do in Northern countries, with a multitude of small bundles and an air of patient submission to authority – and sailors returning from leave. We slept fitfully, jolting and stopping, changed once in the night, slept again and awoke in an empty carriage, with pine woods passing the windows and the distant view of mountain peaks. New uniforms at the frontier, coffee and bread at the station buffet, people round us of Southern grace and gaiety; on again into the plains, conifers changing to vine and olive, a change of trains at Milan; garlic sausage, bread, and a flask of Orvieto bought from a trolley (we had spent all our money, save for a few francs, in Paris); the sun mounted high and the country glowed with heat; the carriage filled with peasants, ebbing and flowing at each station, the smell of garlic was overwhelming in the hot carriage. At last in the evening we arrived at Venice.

A sombre figure was there to meet us. 'Papa's valet, Plender.'

'I met the express,' said Plender. 'His Lordship thought you must have looked up the train wrong. This seemed only to come from Milan.'

'We travelled third.'

Plender tittered politely. 'I have the gondola here. I shall follow with the luggage in the *vaporetto.*'

· · · · ·

He led us to the waiting boat. The gondoliers wore green and white livery and silver plaques on their chests; they smiled and bowed.

'*Palazzo. Pronto.*'

'*Sì, signore Plender.*'

And we floated away.

Notes

sought: (from *seek*) tried
Brideshead and Cordelia: Sebastian's elder brother and younger sister, who had been at home
the tents were struck: the tents were taken down
on the show ground: there had been a farm show at Brideshead
trampled: crushed by being walked on
his injury: Sebastian had broken a bone in his foot
sleeper: a bed on a train
Dunkirk: a port on the French coast
the Lotti: a Paris hotel

Foyot's: a smart restaurant
loitered: strolled around
Gare de Lyon: the Paris station for trains heading south
Orvieto: Italian wine
tittered: laughed nervously
gondola: a boat used on the canals in Venice
vaporetto: a steam-powered passenger boat
plaques: badges
Palazzo. Pronto. (Italian) To the palace, at once
Sì, signore Plender: (Italian) Yes, Mr Plender

Comprehension

The author

Decide whether these statements are true (**T**) or false (**F**).

1 Evelyn Waugh's main interest was in teaching.
2 His first novel was *A Handful of Dust*.
3 He became a Roman Catholic in his late twenties.
4 He wrote a well-known trilogy of World War I novels.
5 However, he is most famous for his travel writing.
6 He finally settled in the south-east of England.

The text

A Match these words from the text with their meanings.

1	frontier (line 22)	a	very strong
2	buffet (line 23)	b	uniform
3	conifers (line 23)	c	snack-bar
4	peasants (line 27)	d	pine trees
5	overwhelming (line 27)	e	serious-looking
6	sombre (line 29)	f	border
7	valet (line 29)	g	manservant
8	livery (line 35)	h	country people

B Rewrite these phrases or sentences in your own words.

1 in leisurely fashion (line 6)

2 We can both travel third for that (line 11)
3 with a multitude of small bundles (line 18)
4 (with) an air of patient submission to authority (line 19)
5 returning from leave (line 19)
6 We slept fitfully (line 20)
7 all our money save for a few francs (line 25)
8 ebbing and flowing at each station (line 27)

C Answer these questions.

1 What does Charles mean when he says Sebastian 'was like a friend made on board ship' (line 2)?
2 What is Sebastian's 'home port' (line 3)?
3 Why do you think 'the lawyers' (line 10) pay for Sebastian?
4 How do we know from the text that they are travelling the cheapest possible way?
5 How do they spend their day in Paris?
6 Why don't they sleep very well on the train from Paris?
7 Why are there 'new uniforms at the frontier' (line 22)?
8 How does the author show us that Charles and Sebastian are moving from the north to the south of Europe?
9 Why were they expected to arrive on the express?
10 Who is 'His Lordship' (line 30)?
11 How do they travel from the station?
12 What kind of experience do you think the journey and arrival in Venice is for Charles?

Discussion

1 What impression does the author give of Sebastian by using sea language (line 3)? Why do you think Sebastian wanted 'to keep Charles apart from the rest of his life'?

2 'People round us of Southern grace and gaiety' (line 23). Do you think that people who live in southern Europe are generally more outgoing and sociable than those who live in the north? Do you think that climate affects our personalities?

Role-play

Student A: You are planning a month's holiday travelling around Europe with your friend (Student B). You want to keep the trip as cheap as possible, and suggest travelling overnight by train, with no sleepers, and staying occasionally in youth hostels.

Student B: You are keen to go on the trip, but you don't want it to be too uncomfortable. You are in favour of travelling by train or coach during the daytime, so that you can admire the scenery. You think you should spend a few nights in small hotels, which offer better facilities than youth hostels.

Extension

Vocabulary

'Plender tittered politely' (line 33). Match these ways of smiling or laughing with their definitions.

1	giggle	a	to laugh loudly, sometimes rudely
2	chuckle	b	to smile broadly
3	cackle	c	to laugh nervously or foolishly
4	guffaw	d	to laugh softly or to yourself
5	grin	e	to smile scornfully or self-confidently
6	smirk	f	to laugh noisily in a high voice

Now put them correctly into these sentences. Use each verb only once.

1 The schoolgirls .... nervously as they waited for the examiner.

2 'They'll never catch up with me now!' thought John, and he .... quietly to himself as the plane took off.

3 'Don't worry, you'll be a great success,' said Diana, ... at me to give me confidence.

4 'Look at what you've done, you silly girl!' .... the old woman. 'That's the funniest thing I've seen for years!'

5 'I'm afraid the manager has heard about your unpunctuality, Lee,' said Mrs Hodgson, ... unpleasantly.

6 The men at the bar .... loudly at each other's jokes.

Grammar

'I think you'd better come with me ...' (line 8). Choose the correct ending for each sentence.

1	I'd rather	A	go by boat.
2	He ought	B	to going by boat.
3	They're looking forward	C	to go by boat.
4	We promised	D	going by boat.
5	She enjoys	E	in going by boat.
6	He objected	F	on going by boat
7	She always used		
8	I insisted		
9	We succeeded		
10	These days he's used		

Composition (120 – 180 words)

Write a description of a recent journey you have made. Describe your fellow travellers, and any interesting incidents which occurred.

25

GRAHAM GREENE

1904 – 1991

Graham Greene was born in Berkhamsted, in Hertfordshire, England, the son of a schoolmaster. He was educated at his father's school and Oxford University, and then worked as a reporter for *The Times*. In 1927 he married and became a Roman Catholic. He started writing poetry, and then novels, and contributed regularly to the leading literary magazines and newspapers of the time. He worked at the Foreign Office during World War II, and based some episodes in his books on his wartime experiences.

Greene is one of the best-known writers of the twentieth century. His work is most admired for its compelling themes and the powerful quality of its writing. He is first and foremost a great story-teller, writing economically but creating a believable atmosphere every time. His short stories are masterpieces of short fiction.

Greene's novels fall into two categories: the lighter action novels he called entertainments, and the serious novels whose themes include religion and guilt. He became increasingly interested in Catholic ideas of good and evil, which are reflected in his later novels. He also wrote travel books, plays and children's books.

Well-known works by Graham Greene include: *Stamboul Train* (1932), *Brighton Rock* (1938), *The Power and the Glory* (1940), *The Heart of the Matter* (1948), *The Third Man* (1950), *The End of the Affair* (1951), *The Quiet American* (1955), *A Burnt-Out Case* (1961), *The Honorary Consul* (1973).

The Third Man

This novel was originally written as a film script, and made into a very famous film. The story is set in post-war Vienna, which is controlled by four powers, France, Britain, Russia and America.

Rollo Martins, a writer of paperback Westerns, is invited to Vienna by an old friend, Harry Lime. But when he arrives, he discovers that Lime has been killed in a car accident. Martins attends his friend's funeral, where he hears that Lime was involved in black market deals. Reluctant to believe this of his friend, Martins decides to find out the truth about Lime's sudden death. In his search for the truth, he meets Lime's neighbours, Herr Koch and his wife Ilse, who seem a little nervous about answering questions. All that Martins knows (or thinks he knows) is that Lime was knocked down and carried into the house by two people ...

'Did you tell me that you had actually seen the accident?'

Herr Koch exchanged glances with his wife. 'The inquest is over, Ilse. There is no harm. You can trust my judgement. The gentleman is a friend. Yes, I saw the accident, but you are the only one who knows. When I say that I saw it, perhaps I should say that I heard it. I heard the brakes put on and the sound of the skid, and I got to the window in time to see them carry the body to the house.'

'But didn't you give evidence?'

'It is better not to be mixed up in such things. My office cannot spare me. We are short of staff, and of course I did not actually *see* –'

'But you told me yesterday how it happened.'

'That was how they described it in the papers.'

'Was he in great pain?'

'He was dead. I looked right down from my window here and I saw his face. I know when a man is dead. You see, it is, in a way, my business. I am the head clerk at the mortuary.'

'But the others say that he did not die at once.'

'Perhaps they don't know death as well as I do.'

'He was dead, of course, when the doctor arrived. He told me that.'

'He was dead at once. You can take the word of a man who knows.'

'I think, Herr Koch, that you should have given evidence.'

'One must look after oneself, Herr Martins. I was not the only one who should have been there.'

'How do you mean?'

'There were three people who helped to carry your friend to the house.'

'I know – two men and the driver.'

'The driver stayed where he was. He was very much shaken, poor man.'

'Three men ...' It was as though suddenly, fingering that bare wall, his fingers had encountered, not so much a crack perhaps, but at least a roughness that had not been smoothed away by the careful builders.

'Can you describe the men?'

But Herr Koch was not trained to observe the living: only the man with the toupee had attracted his eyes – the other two were just men, neither tall nor short, thick nor thin. He had seen them from far above, foreshortened, bent over their burden; they had not looked up, and he had quickly looked away and closed the window, realizing at once the wisdom of not being seen himself.

'There was no evidence I could really give, Herr Martins.'

No evidence, Martins thought, no evidence! • • • And the third man? Who was he?

Notes *actually:* in fact
inquest: a legal inquiry to discover why a person died
skid: losing control of a car
give evidence: appear in court as a witness
mortuary: a place where dead bodies are kept before they are buried

shaken: shocked, upset
encountered: met, found
toupee: a small wig to cover a bald spot, usually for a man
foreshortened: appearing smaller than they really were
their burden: what they had to carry

Comprehension

The author

Only one ending in each group is correct. Choose the correct one.

1 Graham Greene worked
   a at his father's school. c at Oxford University.
   b for *The Times*. d for the Roman
   Catholic Church.

2 He started his writing career with
   a thrillers. c poetry.
   b film scripts. d newspaper articles.

3 During World War II he
   a fought in the army.
   b travelled widely.
   c became a Roman Catholic.
   d worked for the Foreign Office.

4 He always wrote
   a believable stories. c on religious themes.
   b action novels. d fiction.

The text

Answer these questions.

1 Why does Herr Koch 'exchange glances with his wife' (line 2) and try to reassure her?
2 Did Herr Koch see the accident?
3 What kind of accident was it, from his description?
4 What did he see from the window?
5 What are the reasons he offers for not giving evidence? What do you think his real reason is?
6 Why is Herr Koch sure that Harry Lime was dead?

7 Who do you think 'the others' (line 16) are?
8 Who told Martins that Harry was dead when the doctor arrived?
9 Martins criticizes Herr Koch. Why?
10 How many people had helped to carry the body to the house after the accident?
11 How many people do you think there were at the scene of the accident?
12 What is the 'crack' or 'roughness' that Martins thinks he has found (line 28)?
13 What do you know about the men who carried the body away?
14 Why didn't Herr Koch observe them very well?
15 Why did Herr Koch close the window quickly?
16 Who does Martins' final question refer to?

Discussion

1 There is an air of mystery and secrecy about this passage. Do you think Martins will be able to find out the truth about his friend? Do you think it is safe for him to go on asking questions? Or is Herr Koch right when he says 'It is better not to be mixed up in such things'? What dangers are involved, do you think?

2 Can you explain the title of the book, *The Third Man*? How important is the third man referred to in this text? What effect do you think he might have on the development of the story?

3 How important are your friends to you? Do you think it is better to have one or two really good friends, or many friends you don't know quite so well?

Role-play

Student A: You are a police detective and you are interviewing a witness to a bank robbery (Student B). Try to find out as many details as you can, but make sure the witness only tells you about what he/she actually saw. Be polite but firm!

Student B: You want to help the police but you can't remember very much about the robbery. Explain where you were and what you were doing. You think you can describe one of the robbers fairly well, but not the other two. You are rather nervous, as you've never had anything to do with the police before!

Extension

Vocabulary

A 'But didn't you give evidence?' (line 7). Complete these sentences with the correct legal vocabulary: *lawyer sentence verdict prosecuted jury acquitted fine statement accused.*

1 The .... came back into court to give their ....
2 The .... was convicted and given a ten-year jail ....
3 However, his brother was found not guilty and was ....
4 The woman was .... for shoplifting, and had to pay a heavy ....
5 The defence .... read out a .... from his client.

B 'Fingering that bare wall' (line 27). Complete the sentences, using these parts of the body as verbs: *eye hand toe head nose elbow thumb finger.*

1 The sports car .... its way into the busy traffic.

2 Although we warned her it might be dangerous, she decided to .... a lift on the road.
3 From now on you'll have to do what the boss tells you, and .... the line.
4 The fat woman .... her way rudely to the front of the queue.
5 She .... the bank notes lovingly as she counted them.
6 The children .... the cakes hungrily.
7 We set off at dawn, and .... for Scotland.
8 John looked rather worried as he .... me the letter.

Word-building

'The wisdom of not being seen himself' (line 35). Complete these sentences with the correct noun ending in *-dom*, *-hood* or *-ship*.

1 I have many happy memories of my child........... .
2 Unfortunately, frequent quarrels destroyed their relation..........., and they had to split up.
3 The monarch rules over his king........... .
4 How many young couples live in your neighbour...........?
5 I greatly value his friend........... .
6 Parent........... has changed him and made him much more responsible.

Composition (120 – 180 words)

The police have asked you to write a report of a car accident which you saw. Explain what you were doing at the time, describe where the accident happened, how many people and vehicles were involved, whose fault you think it was, and what happened next.

26

JOHN WYNDHAM

1903 – 1969

John Wyndham is the pen-name of John Wyndham Harris, who was born in Knowle in Warwickshire, England, the son of a barrister.

In his childhood he was an admirer of H. G. Wells and Jules Verne, two of the earliest writers of science fiction. He followed several different careers (farming, law, commercial art, advertising) before settling down to write science fiction, although he preferred to call his work 'logical fantasy'.

At first he wrote short stories, which were published in popular magazines. Then he became famous with his first novel, *The Day of the Triffids*.

Most of Wyndham's work shows how people respond to a sudden disaster, usually caused by something abnormal or supernatural. There is often a striking contrast between the event and its peaceful English background. Several of his novels have been filmed.

Well-known works by John Wyndham include: *The Day of the Triffids* (1951), *The Kraken Wakes* (1953), *The Chrysalids* (1955), *The Midwich Cuckoos* (1957), *The Seeds of Time* (1969).

The Day of the Triffids

A strange disaster has struck an unsuspecting world. All over the planet, people have been blinded by what seemed to be a particularly beautiful display of shooting stars in the sky. Now only a handful of people are able to see, and as a result there is chaos. This is made much worse by the invasion of large numbers of threatening plants called triffids. They are two metres high and move around on three-pronged roots. If they sting someone, he or she usually dies, and a blind person is an easy target.

Bill, the narrator, is one of the few people left who can see. He is exploring the countryside south of London, hoping to find his girlfriend, Josella, and other sighted people who can fight the triffids with him.

I was almost clear of the place when a small figure bounded out of one of the last garden gates and came running up the road towards me, waving both arms. I pulled up, looking around for triffids in a way that was becoming instinctive, picked up my gun, and climbed down.

5 The child was dressed in a blue cotton frock, white socks, and sandals. She looked about nine or ten years old. A pretty little girl – I could see that even though her dark brown curls were now uncared for, and her face dirtied with smeared tears. She pulled at my sleeve.

'Please, please,' she said, urgently, 'please come and see what's happened to
10 Tommy.'

I stood staring down at her. The awful loneliness of the day lifted. My mind seemed to break out of the case I had made for it. I wanted to pick her up and hold her to me. I could feel tears close behind my eyes. I held out my hand to her, and she took it. Together we walked back to the gate through which she had gone.

15 'Tommy's there,' she said, pointing.

A little boy about four years of age lay on the diminutive patch of lawn between the flower-beds. It was quite obvious at a glance why he was there.

'The *thing* hit him,' she said. 'It hit him and he fell down. And it wanted to hit me when I tried to help him. Horrible *thing!*'

20 I looked up and saw the top of a triffid rising above the fence that bordered the garden.

'Put your hands over your ears. I'm going to make a bang,' I said.

She did so, and I blasted the top off the triffid.

'Horrible *thing*,' she repeated. 'Is it dead now?'

25 I was about to assure her that it was when it began to rattle the little sticks against its stem, just as the one at Steeple Honey had done. As then, I gave it the other barrel to shut it up.

'Yes,' I said. 'It's dead now.'

We walked across to the little boy. The scarlet slash of the sting was vivid on his pale
30 cheek. It must have happened some hours before. She knelt beside him.

'It isn't any good,' I told her, gently.

She looked up, fresh tears in her eyes.

'Is Tommy dead, too?'

I squatted down beside her, and shook my head.

35 'I'm afraid he is.'

After a while she said:

'Poor Tommy! Will we bury him – like the puppies?'

'Yes,' I told her.

In all the overwhelming disaster that was the only grave I dug – and it was a very
40 small one. She gathered a little bunch of flowers, and laid them on top of it. Then we drove away.

Notes	clear of the place: out of the village		Steeple Honey: a place where Bill had been previously

Notes
clear of the place: out of the village
bounded: ran with big strides
pulled up: stopped (in a vehicle)
frock: a dress
smeared: rubbed with dirt
diminutive: very small
blasted: shot
rattle: shake and make a noise (this is what triffids do just before they sting people)

Steeple Honey: a place where Bill had been previously
the other barrel: Bill's gun has two barrels (for storing and firing ammunition)
scarlet slash: bright red line or mark
vivid: bright, clearly seen
squatted: crouched down on the backs of my heels
puppies: young dogs
overwhelming: too great to resist
grave: a hole in the ground for burying a dead body

Comprehension

The author

Complete these sentences in your own words.

1 John Wyndham's father ....
2 John Wyndham only became a writer after ....
3 When he was a child, he liked ....
4 He did not like calling ....
5 In addition to novels, he ....

The text

A Answer these questions.

1 Why do you think the little girl's hair looks 'uncared for' (line 7)?
2 Why do you think she has been crying?
3 How does Bill feel when the child speaks to him? Why do you think he feels like that?
4 What do you think the connection is between the child and Tommy?
5 What is 'the *thing*' (line 18)?
6 How does the child feel about 'the *thing*'?
7 How did Tommy die?
8 What do you think the triffid behind the fence would have done if Bill hadn't killed it?
9 Is a triffid easy to kill? Why, or why not?
10 What do you think happened to Bill at Steeple Honey?
11 How does the child feel about Tommy's death?
12 What do you think happened to 'the puppies' (line 37)?
13 Other people have already died. Why do you think Bill hasn't buried anyone yet?

B Rewrite these phrases or sentences in your own words.

1 looking around for triffids in a way that was becoming instinctive (line 3)
2 The awful loneliness of the day lifted (line 11)
3 My mind seemed to break out of the case I had made for it (line 11)
4 It was quite obvious at a glance (line 17)
5 As then, I gave it the other barrel to shut it up (line 26)

Discussion

1 What do you think has happened to the child's family? Where do you think she and Bill will go now?

2 Imagine what happens next. Does Bill find his girlfriend? Do they manage to beat the triffids in the end?

3 What would you do now if you were Bill? Would you go abroad to see if other countries had been attacked by the triffids? Would you go back to London to set up a new administration network for all the reorganization that would be needed? Would you travel as far away from the triffids as possible, to a Scottish island perhaps, and try to live independently there, growing your own food? Or would you stay and try to help all the blind people?

4 Can you believe a story like this? Do you enjoy science fiction? Why, or why not?

Extension

Vocabulary

'Like the puppies' (line 37). Match the animal on the left with its young on the right.

1	horse	a	duckling
2	cat	b	fawn
3	cow	c	chick
4	fox	d	piglet
5	goat	e	foal
6	sheep	f	kid
7	duck	g	kitten
8	hen	h	calf
9	deer	i	lamb
10	pig	j	cub

Grammar

'I'm going to make a bang' (line 22). Use a correct future form in the following sentences. Sometimes more than one form is possible.

1 If she gets a visa, she (be able) to go to Canada.
2 I promise I (come) to see you off at the airport.
3 This weekend he (take) his cousin to the theatre.
4 Was that the doorbell? Don't worry, I (answer) it.
5 I hope she (pass) her exam next month.
6 Watch out! That dog (run) into the water.
7 This time next year she (work) in France.
8 I think Peter (leave) by the time you get here.

Conjunctions

'I could see that even though her dark brown curls ....' (line 6). Complete the second sentence so that it means the same as the one before.

1 Although she was ill, she kept on working.
  Despite ....
2 I didn't get the job, but I don't regret applying for it.
  Even though ....

3 She didn't tell him the news. However, he heard it from someone else.
  Although ....
4 The weather was terrible that day, but we still went for a swim.
  In spite of ....
5 Although I don't like him, I must admit he's good at his job.
  I don't like him, ...

Phrasal verbs

'I looked up and saw the top of a triffid' (line 20). Complete the phrasal verbs with *look* in these sentences.

1 If you don't know his number, you'd better look it .... in the phone book.
2 When she starts her new job, she'll have to look .... a flat in Manchester.
3 Look ....! There's a train coming! Don't stand so close to the edge of the platform.
4 Shall we look .... the British Museum before we have lunch?
5 Could you just look .... my essay and check that I haven't made too many mistakes?
6 Would you mind looking .... the children while I go shopping?

Composition (120 – 180 words)

On a recent trip to a distant part of your country, you are sure you saw aliens/triffids/UFOs. Write a report about what you experienced, to be sent to the authorities. Give detailed descriptions, and suggest a possible course of action.

27

WILLIAM GOLDING

1911 – 1993

William Golding was born near Newquay in Cornwall, England. He was educated at Marlborough School and Oxford University, and worked as a writer, actor, producer, then teacher. After serving in the Royal Navy during World War II, he returned to teaching until 1960. He published some poetry, but it was not until the publication of his first novel, *Lord of the Flies*, that he became famous.

Golding wrote radio plays, short stories and several novels. Although he won the Nobel Prize for Literature in 1983, his best-known work is still *Lord of the Flies*. The main theme in all his writing is man's tendency towards evil, which is at its most obvious when, as in many of his novels, characters are put into an isolated, stressful situation.

Well-known works by William Golding include: *Lord of the Flies* (1954), *Pincher Martin* (1956), *Free Fall* (1959), *The Pyramid* (1967), *Darkness Visible* (1979), *Rites of Passage* (1980), *The Paper Men* (1984).

Lord of the Flies

In this modern classic, which E. M. Forster described as 'beautifully written, tragic and provocative', Golding takes the characters from *Coral Island*, a nineteenth-century children's classic by R. M. Ballantyne, and shows how circumstances bring out the evil in them.

At the beginning of the book, a group of schoolboys are stranded on an uninhabited tropical island, after the plane in which they are travelling is shot down. One of them, a confident twelve-year-old called Ralph, meets Piggy, who is about the same age, but fat and often ill. They do not yet know how many of their companions have survived, or how serious the situation is. For the moment they are both enjoying the sun, the sea and the freedom.

In this extract, Piggy opens the conversation by admiring Ralph's swimming.

'You can't half swim well.'

Ralph paddled backwards down the slope, immersed his mouth and blew a jet of water into the air. Then he lifted his chin and spoke.

'I could swim when I was five. Daddy taught me. He's a commander in the Navy. When he gets leave he'll come and rescue us. What's your father?'

Piggy flushed suddenly.

'My dad's dead,' he said quickly, 'and my mum –'

He took off his glasses and looked vainly for something with which to clean them.

'I used to live with my auntie. She kept a sweet-shop. I used to get ever so many sweets. As many as I liked. When'll your dad rescue us?'

'Soon as he can.'

Piggy rose dripping from the water and stood naked, cleaning his glasses with a sock. The only sound that reached them now through the heat of the morning was the long, grinding roar of the breakers on the reef.

'How does he know we're here?'

Ralph lolled in the water. • • •

'How does he know we're here?'

Because, thought Ralph, because, because. The roar from the reef became very distant.

'They'd tell him at the airport.'

Piggy shook his head, put on his flashing glasses and looked down at Ralph.

'Not them. Didn't you hear what the pilot said? About the atom bomb? They're all dead.'

Ralph pulled himself out of the water, stood facing Piggy, and considered this unusual problem.

Piggy persisted.

'This an island, isn't it?'

'I climbed a rock,' said Ralph slowly, 'and I think this is an island.'

'They're all dead,' said Piggy, 'an' this is an island. Nobody don't know we're here. Your dad don't know, nobody don't know –'

His lips quivered and the spectacles were dimmed with mist.

'We may stay here till we die.'

• • • • •

'Get my clothes,' muttered Ralph. 'Along there.'

He trotted through the sand, enduring the sun's enmity, crossed the platform and found his scattered clothes. To put on a grey shirt once more was strangely pleasing. Then he climbed the edge of the platform and sat in the green shade on a convenient trunk. Piggy hauled himself up, carrying most of his clothes under his arms. Then he sat carefully on a fallen trunk near the little cliff that fronted the lagoon; and the tangled reflections quivered over him.

Presently he spoke.

'We got to find the others. We got to do something.'

Notes	paddled: (here) moved in the water by using his hands	This an island: (ungrammatical) This is an island
	commander: an officer	Nobody don't know: (ungrammatical) Nobody knows
	the Navy: the British sea defence force	Your dad don't know: (ungrammatical) Your father
	gets leave: gets permission, or time off work	doesn't know
	dad, mum, auntie: familiar forms for father, mother, aunt	Get my clothes: (short for) I'll get my clothes
	grinding: a powerful noise, like stone on stone	enmity: hatred, harshness
	breakers: high waves that break on the shore	platform: (here) high flat rocks
	reef: a ridge of rock near the surface of the water	lagoon: a salt-water lake near the sea
	lolled: relaxed lazily	tangled: confused, mixed up
		We got to: (ungrammatical) We've got to

Comprehension

The author

See how much you can remember. Answer these questions quickly without referring to page 111.

1 Where was Golding born?
2 Which university did he go to?
3 What did he do in World War II?
4 What is his best-known book?
5 When did he win the Nobel Prize for Literature?
6 What is the main theme of his writing?

The text

A Match these verbs from the text with their meanings.

1	immersed (line 2)	a	spoke quietly
2	flushed (line 6)	b	walked quickly
3	quivered (line 31)	c	pulled with difficulty
4	muttered (line 33)	d	(his face) went red
5	trotted (line 34)	e	put completely into the water
6	hauled (line 37)	f	trembled, shook

B Rewrite these phrases or sentences in your own words.

1 You can't half swim well (line 1)
2 What's your father? (line 5)
3 (he) looked vainly for something (line 8)
4 She kept a sweet-shop (line 9)

5 Piggy rose ... from the water (line 12)
6 Piggy persisted (line 26)
7 enduring the sun's enmity (line 34)
8 (he) found his scattered clothes (line 35)

C Answer these questions.

1 Why does Ralph swim so well?
2 Why does Piggy 'flush suddenly' (line 6)?
3 Why did Piggy live with his aunt, do you think?
4 Why do you think he mentions that he used to get as many sweets as he liked?
5 How do you know it is hot on the island?
6 What is Piggy worried about?
7 'They're all dead' (line 22). Who do you think 'they' refers to?
8 Why are Piggy's spectacles 'dimmed with mist' (line 31)?
9 How does Ralph feel about putting his clothes on again?
10 Why is the trunk (line 37) convenient?

Discussion

1 What can you find out about the two boys' characters from the text? How different are they? Do you feel sorry for either of them? Why, or why not? Do you think one of them might become a leader if they find the other boys? If so, which one, and why?

2 Imagine how the story might develop. Will Piggy and Ralph find the other boys? How will they manage to live on this tropical island? Will they be rescued eventually?

Role-play

Student A: You and your friends (Students B and C) have been shipwrecked on a desert island. You think the important thing is to be rescued as soon as possible, so you suggest keeping a fire going permanently. (The smoke would be seen by the crew of any passing ship or plane.)

Student B: You don't want to waste time on rescue plans. You feel the first thing to do is to make a shelter in case it rains, then to find fresh water and fruit to eat. Explain to your friends that it could be a long time before you are rescued. Try to work out a plan of what should be done every day to make life on the island more comfortable.

Student C: You are enjoying sunbathing and swimming – it's like a free holiday. You can't understand why your friends are making such a fuss. You feel sure someone will come and rescue you soon. Until then, everybody should relax!

Extension

Vocabulary

A Put these words from the text into new sentences of your own: *rescue dripping roar shook unusual climbed quivered shade cliff island.*

B 'Get my clothes,' muttered Ralph (line 33). Complete each sentence with one of these ways of talking: *speak discuss whisper mention scream say argue chat.*

1 I told him to be quiet, so he didn't .... a word.

2 How many languages do you ....?

3 I know he's sensitive about his illness, so I didn't .... it.

4 'Quiet! Don't let anyone hear us!' she .... in my ear.

5 I'm not here on business. I just popped in for a ....

6 I can see you don't agree with me, so we'd better .... it.

7 Just as Stuart entered the house, he heard a long, high-pitched .... coming from one of the upstairs rooms.

8 Don't .... with me! Just hurry up and do what I tell you!

Phrasal verbs

'He took off his glasses' (line 8). Complete the phrasal verbs with *take* in these sentences.

1 He takes .... his father: they're both extremely intelligent.

2 If we expand our business, we'll have to take .... more staff.

3 I'm afraid I didn't really take .... Frieda at our first meeting, but now I really like her.

4 He's planning to take ....sailing when he retires.

5 I'm sorry, I take .... what I said. I was quite wrong.

6 The plane won't be able to take .... in this thick fog.

7 We all believed his story, but I'm afraid we were taken ....

8 Yes, I'm the new manager. I took .... from Mrs Johnson on Monday.

Composition (120 – 180 words)

Write a composition describing three objects you would like to take with you to a desert island. Explain how each of them would be useful to you, or make your life pleasanter.

28

GERALD DURRELL

1925 – 1995

Gerald Durrell was born in Jamshedpur, India, and was educated by private tutors, with a special emphasis on natural history. From the beginning he was interested in zoology and wildlife. For six years he lived with his family on the Mediterranean island of Corfu, where he kept animals and observed the wildlife. He became a student keeper for the famous Whipsnade Zoo in Bedfordshire, England, but soon began to organize, finance and lead expeditions for collecting zoological specimens to many lesser-known parts of the world.

In 1959 he created his own zoo in Jersey in the Channel Islands, later forming the Jersey Wildlife Preservation Trust, which took over the zoo. Subsequently he established Wildlife Preservation Trust International, which now has thousands of members worldwide and is a flourishing organization. He made many wildlife films for television.

Although Gerald Durrell is well known for his popular accounts of animal life, his books are also appreciated for their gentle humour and detailed descriptions of people and places. His best-known book is *My Family and Other Animals*.

Well-known works by Gerald Durrell include: *The Overloaded Ark* (1953), *My Family and Other Animals* (1956), *A Zoo in My Luggage* (1960), *The Whispering Land* (1961), *Island Zoo* (1961), *Birds, Beasts and Relatives* (1969), *The Garden of the Gods* (1978).

My Family and Other Animals

This book is an account of the author's childhood in Corfu. It describes not only the wildlife which so fascinated him as a small boy, but also the eccentric characters to be found on the island and in the Durrell family. Gerald's mother, eldest brother Larry, another brother Leslie, and sister Margo all have their own ways of enjoying life.

In this extract, the family have only just arrived in Corfu, and are settling into a rented villa.

As soon as we had settled down and started to enjoy the island, Larry, with characteristic generosity, wrote to all his friends and asked them to come out and stay. The fact that the villa was only just big enough to house the family apparently had not occurred to him.

'I've asked a few people out for a week or so,' he said casually to Mother one morning.

. . . . .

'You'd better let the Pension Suisse know when they're coming,' Mother remarked.

'What for?' asked Larry, surprised.

'So they can reserve the rooms,' said Mother, equally surprised.

'But I've invited them to stay here,' Larry pointed out.

'Larry! You haven't! Really, you are most *thoughtless*. How can they possibly stay here?'

'I really don't see what you're making a fuss about,' said Larry coldly.

'But where are they going to *sleep?*' said Mother, distraught. 'There's hardly enough room for us, as it is.'

'Nonsense, Mother, there's plenty of room if the place is organized properly. If Margo and Les sleep out on the veranda, that gives you two rooms; you and Gerry could move into the drawing-room, and that would leave those rooms free.'

'Don't be silly, dear. We can't all camp out all over the place like gypsies. Besides, it's still chilly at night, and I don't think Margo and Les ought to sleep outside. There simply isn't room to entertain in this villa. You'll just have to write to these people and put them off.'

'I can't put them off,' said Larry, 'they're on their way.'

'Really, Larry, you are the most annoying creature. Why on earth didn't you tell me before? You wait until they're nearly here, and then you tell me.'

'I didn't know you were going to treat the arrival of a few friends as if it was a major catastrophe,' Larry explained.

'But, dear, it's so silly to invite people when you know there's no room in the villa.'

'I do wish you'd stop fussing,' said Larry irritably; 'there's quite a simple solution to the whole business.'

'What?' asked Mother suspiciously.

'Well, since the villa isn't big enough, let's move to one that is.'

'Don't be ridiculous. Whoever heard of moving into a larger house because you've invited some friends to stay?'

'What's the matter with the idea? It seems a perfectly sensible solution to me; after all, if you say there's no room here, the obvious thing to do is to move.'

'The obvious thing to do is not to invite people,' said Mother severely.

'I don't think it's good for us to live like hermits,' said Larry. 'I only really invited them for you. They're a charming crowd. I thought you'd like to have them. Liven things up a bit for you.'

'I'm quite lively enough, thank you,' said Mother with dignity.

> **Notes**
> *casually:* as if it wasn't planned
> *Pension Suisse:* the local hotel or guest-house
> *distraught:* distressed, very worried
> *veranda:* a covered platform along the side of the house
> *drawing-room:* (old-fashioned) a living-room
> *gypsies:* a race of travelling people
> *put them off:* arrange for them to come another time
> *catastrophe:* a disaster, a sudden terrible event
>
> *fussing:* making trouble about it
> *irritably:* with annoyance
> *suspiciously:* not trusting him
> *ridiculous:* silly, stupid
> *severely:* harshly, critically
> *hermits:* people who live completely alone
> *Liven things up:* (short for) They'll make life more fun
> *with dignity:* proudly

Comprehension

The author

Only one ending in each group is correct. Choose the correct one.

1 Gerald Durrell lives in
   a India. b Corfu. c London. d Jersey.

2 He became interested in zoology
   a when he was very young.
   b when he worked at Whipsnade.
   c when he lived in Corfu.
   d when he moved to Jersey.

3 The zoo which he created
   a was taken over by a trust.
   b has thousands of visitors every week.
   c is twenty-five years old.
   d is in Bedfordshire.

4 He has
   a acted in several films.
   b made a lot of wildlife films.
   c made a film about Jersey.
   d written several film scripts.

The text

A Match these words from the text with their opposites.

1 generosity (line 2)   a departure
2 casually (line 5)   b deliberately
3 thoughtless (line 11)   c charming

4 distraught (line 14)   d considerate
5 annoying (line 24)   e relaxed
6 arrival (line 26)   f meanness
7 major (line 26)   g foolish
8 sensible (line 35)   h minor

B Rewrite these phrases or sentences in your own words.

1 with characteristic generosity (line 1)
2 to come out and stay (line 2)
3 The fact ... had not occurred to him (line 3)
4 I really don't see what you're making a fuss about (line 13)
5 as it is (line 15)
6 We can't all camp out all over the place (line 19)
7 to entertain (line 21)
8 They're a charming crowd (line 39)

C Answer these questions.

1 What do we learn about Larry's character in the first sentence? Do you think the author is laughing at his eldest brother?
2 What does the author tell us about the size of the villa?
3 Why does Mother mention the Pension Suisse?
4 Why is Larry surprised by this?
5 What is the problem that Mother is worried about?
6 What solution does Larry first suggest?
7 Why is that not acceptable to Mother?

8 What does Mother say to show that she is cross with Larry?

9 What is Larry's next suggestion?

10 What reason does he give for inviting friends to stay? Do you think it is the real reason?

Discussion

1 What do you think the family will do next? Will they 'camp out' and let the visitors stay in the villa? Or book the visitors into a hotel? Or move to a new villa? Which solution would you choose?

2 What do you think of Larry's character? Is he selfish or not?

3 When a number of people have to share a house or a flat, do you think there should be rules (for example, not inviting visitors unless parents agree)? What kind of rules do you or did you have at home? Why?

Role-play

Student A: You and your friend (Student B) are planning a party for your eighteenth birthday. You would like to have it at your parents' house, but you haven't asked them yet. Think what you will have to arrange, if the party is at your house.

Student B: You think it's better to invite people to a restaurant for the party. It will cost more, but perhaps it will be more fun. And you won't have to clear up afterwards!

Extension

Grammar

A 'I do wish you'd stop fussing' (line 29). Make correct sentences for the following situations, starting with *I wish*.

1 I'm sorry I can't come to the ceremony.
2 He talks far too much, doesn't he?

3 What a pity I can't speak Greek!
4 I'd like to go out, but it's still raining.
5 It's about time he made up his mind.
6 You might do some work for a change!
7 Things would be much better if I had a car.
8 I don't know why she doesn't phone me.

B 'There's plenty of room' (line 16). Circle the words in this list which are uncountable: *furniture books meat fruit people accommodation news children advice vegetables information luggage.*

Now put them into sentences of your own.

C 'A few people ...' (line 5). Complete these sentences with *much, a lot of, few, a few, little* or *a little*. Use each word or phrase only once.

1 Very .... students understood what the lecturer was saying.
2 There is still .... work to be done in the garden.
3 Whether I can go or not depends on how .... money I have.
4 Because she had so .... luggage, she was able to check in for her flight very quickly.
5 I think he's got .... stamps left, but you'd better hurry in case they run out.
6 This dish needs .... salt to bring out the flavour of the meat.

Composition (120 – 180 words)

1 Write Larry's letter to a friend, telling him/her about the Durrells' new home in Corfu, and inviting him/her to come and stay for a few days.

2 Having read pages 115 and 116, can you explain why Gerald Durrell chose the title *My Family and Other Animals*?

3 'Wild animals should never be kept in captivity.' Discuss.

29

AGATHA CHRISTIE

1890 – 1976

Agatha Miller was born in Torquay in Devon, England. Using her first husband's surname, she wrote more than seventy classic detective novels. Her most popular characters are the Belgian detective, Hercule Poirot, and the village spinster, Miss Marple. After her first marriage ended in divorce, she married Max Mallowan, a famous archaeologist and professor at London University. She also wrote many stage plays, and at one time three of her plays were running simultaneously at West End theatres. Her play *The Mousetrap*, which opened in 1952, is still the longest-running play ever performed in London. She also wrote under the name of Mary Westmacott.

Agatha Christie's whodunits are popular throughout the world and have been translated into many languages. Her books achieve larger sales than those of any other single writer except Shakespeare. She is appreciated for her clear, uncomplicated writing style, her ingenious plots and the suspense which she always manages to create.

Well-known works by Agatha Christie include: *The Mysterious Affair at Styles* (1920), *The Murder of Roger Ackroyd* (1926), *Murder at the Vicarage* (1930), *Murder on the Orient Express* (1934), *Death on the Nile* (1937), *And Then There Were None* (1941), *4.50 from Paddington* (1957).

4.50 from Paddington

Mrs McGillicuddy is a sensible, elderly woman. She has been doing her Christmas shopping in London, and is now on the 4.50 train from Paddington station, on her way to visit an old friend, Miss Jane Marple. While looking out of the train window, she sees a frightening sight …

The train gathered speed again. At that moment another train, also on a down-line, swerved inwards towards them, for a moment with almost alarming effect. For a time the two trains ran parallel, now one gaining a little, now the other. Mrs McGillicuddy looked from her window through the windows of the parallel carriages. Most of the blinds were down, but occasionally the occupants of the carriages were visible. The other train was not very full and there were many empty carriages.

At the moment when the two trains gave the illusion of being stationary, a blind in one of the carriages flew up with a snap. Mrs McGillicuddy looked into the lighted first-class carriage that was only a few feet away.

Then she drew her breath in with a gasp and half-rose to her feet.

Standing with his back to the window and to her was a man. His hands were round the throat of a woman who faced him, and he was slowly, remorselessly, strangling her. Her eyes were starting from their sockets, her face was purple and congested. As Mrs McGillicuddy watched fascinated, the end came; the body went limp and crumpled in the man's hands.

At the same moment, Mrs McGillicuddy's train slowed down again and the other began to gain speed. It passed forward and a moment or two later it had vanished from sight.

Almost automatically Mrs McGillicuddy's hand went up to the communication cord, then paused, irresolute. After all, what use would it be ringing the cord of the train in which *she* was travelling? The horror of what she had seen at such close quarters, and the unusual circumstances, made her feel paralysed. *Some* immediate action was necessary – but what?

The door of her compartment was drawn back and a ticket collector said, 'Ticket, please.'

Mrs McGillicuddy turned to him with vehemence.

'A woman has been strangled,' she said. 'In a train that has just passed. I saw it.'

The ticket collector looked at her doubtfully.

'I beg your pardon, madam?'

'A man strangled a woman! In a train. I saw it – through there.' She pointed to the window.

The ticket collector looked extremely doubtful.

'Strangled?' he said disbelievingly.

'Yes, *strangled!* I saw it, I tell you. You must *do* something at once!'

The ticket collector coughed apologetically.

'You don't think, madam, that you may have had a little nap and – er –' he broke off tactfully.

'I have had a nap, but if you think this was a dream, you're quite wrong. I *saw* it, I tell you.'

Notes	
also on a down-line: going in the same direction, away from London	*congested:* swollen with blood
swerved: moved suddenly	*limp:* not stiff
alarming: frightening	*crumpled:* collapsed
stationary: not moving	*communication cord:* if this is pulled, the driver stops the train
snap: a quick movement or noise	*irresolute:* not sure what to do
a few feet: about a metre	*paralysed:* unable to move
remorselessly: without pity	*with vehemence:* firmly, with strong feeling
strangling her: killing her by squeezing her neck	*a little nap:* a short sleep
starting from their sockets: popping out	

Comprehension

The author

See how much you can remember. Answer these questions quickly, without referring back to page 119.

1 Agatha Christie was born ....
2 Her two most famous characters are ....
3 Her second husband was a(n) ....
4 In addition to crime novels, she ....
5 Her books sell in larger quantities ....

The text

A Rewrite these phrases or sentences in your own words.

1 gathered speed (line 1)
2 gaining a little (line 3)
3 occasionally the occupants of the carriages were visible (line 5)
4 gave the illusion of being stationary (line 7)
5 the end came (line 14)
6 it had vanished from sight (line 17)
7 what use would it be (line 20)
8 at such close quarters (line 21)
9 I beg your pardon ...? (line 29)
10 he broke off (line 36)

B Find words in the text ending in -*ly* which have the same meaning as these phrases.

1 without pity
2 before she had even thought about it
3 not sure whether to believe her
4 showing regret for what he is about to say
5 trying to be polite

C Complete these sentences in your own words.

1 The two trains were running ....
2 There were not many people ....
3 Through the window Mrs McGillicuddy saw a man who ....
4 Mrs McGillicuddy did not pull the communication cord because ....
5 The ticket collector did not seem ....
6 But Mrs McGillicuddy insisted ....

Discussion

1 What is so horrifying about what Mrs McGillicuddy has seen? Do you think she's really seen it? Or is the ticket collector right, when he implies she has imagined it?

2 What would you do in her situation?

3 Has she really witnessed a murder? Or can you think of a reasonable explanation for what she has seen, if it wasn't a murder?

4 Imagine what will happen next. Will the police become involved? Will Miss Marple get interested in the event? How could she begin to investigate it?

Extension

Grammar

'*Some* immediate action was necessary' (line 22).
Use *some*, *any* or *no* correctly in these sentences.

1 I don't mind which one you give me. ....
   colour will do.
2 He gave me .... advice which I found quite
   useful.
3 I'm afraid there isn't .... bread left.
4 By the way, have you done .... sailing
   recently?
5 There won't be .... trouble if John's there to
   keep an eye on things.
6 .... sensible person believes everything they
   read in the newspapers.
7 The teacher has only marked .... of the
   homework.
8 .... people are good at cooking, and others
   aren't.

Spelling

'The illusion of being stationary' (line 7). There are
many English words which sound the same but are
spelt differently and have different meanings. Choose
the correct word to complete these sentences.

1 Has my .... order been delivered yet?
   I need more paper urgently.
   (stationary/stationery)
2 With my glasses on, I can see much
   .... than you. (farther/father)
3 The .... flew lower as it approached
   London Airport. (plain/plane)
4 I didn't really like the colour of my pullover, so I
   .... it blue. (dyed/died)
5 I must remember to .... a letter to
   her soon. (right/write)

Sounds

'The ticket collector coughed apologetically'
(line 35). These are all sounds that people make:
cough sniff gasp sneeze snore grunt moan sigh. Put
them into new sentences of your own.

Phrasal verbs

'He broke off tactfully' (line 36). Complete these
sentences with the correct form of a phrasal verb with
break.

1 I was an hour late for the interview because my
   car .... on the motorway.
2 While the Gregsons were away on holiday, thieves
   .... their house and stole several
   valuable antiques.
3 When Jenny discovered her fiancé had lied to her,
   she decided to .... their engagement.
4 Talks between the two delegations
   .... very late last night and will be
   resumed later today.
5 The forest fires which .... recently in
   the province of Malaga may have been started
   deliberately.
6 The store detective tried to hold the woman until
   the manager arrived, but she .... from
   him and ran off.
7 Marcos .... and cried when he heard
   the terrible news.

Composition (120 – 180 words)

1 Write the report that the ticket collector writes
   and hands in to the railway authorities.
2 Write the next three paragraphs in the story, when
   Mrs McGillicuddy tells her friend, Miss Marple,
   about what she saw on the train.

30

P. D. JAMES

1920 –

P. D. James is the pen-name of Phyllis Dorothy White, who was born in Oxford, England, and educated at Cambridge High School. She worked as an administrator for a regional hospital board, and then in the Police Department and Criminal Policy Department of the Home Office, where her experiences provided the background for several of her novels. She is a governor of the BBC and a member of the Arts Council. Her hobbies are exploring churches and walking by the sea.

P. D. James is widely acclaimed for her mastery of the whodunit. Her detective hero, Adam Dalgliesh, and the private investigator, Cordelia Gray, are popular figures in her crime novels. Her books are eagerly awaited and quickly become best sellers. Her plots are detailed and complex, her characters are portrayed with psychological insight, and her writing style is literary and sophisticated. Several of her novels have been televised.

Well-known works by P. D. James include: *Cover Her Face* (1962), *A Mind to Murder* (1963), *Unnatural Causes* (1967), *Shroud for a Nightingale* (1971), *An Unsuitable Job for a Woman* (1972), *The Black Tower* (1975), *Death of an Expert Witness* (1977), *Innocent Blood* (1980), *The Skull Beneath the Skin* (1982), *A Taste for Death* (1986), *Devices and Desires* (1989), *The Children of Men* (1992).

The Skull Beneath the Skin

In this book the young female private detective, Cordelia Gray, is hired to protect an actress, who fears her life will be in danger when she joins a house party on a remote island belonging to the rich and eccentric Ambrose Gorringe. Despite Cordelia's efforts, the actress is in fact murdered, and there is another death on the island before Cordelia finds out who the killer is. This knowledge puts her at risk herself.

In this extract, Cordelia is in a very dangerous situation. She and another visitor to the island, a seventeen-year-old youth called Simon, have been locked in an underground room, which the sea floods completely at high tide. Simon speaks first: he is very weak because he has been imprisoned here for several hours already. Somehow he and Cordelia must escape before the tide rises any higher, otherwise they will drown ...

'Is this death?'

'Perhaps. But there's still a chance. We can swim for it.'

'I'd rather stay here and have you close to me. I don't want to die alone.'

'It's better to die trying. And I won't try without you.'

5 He whispered:

'I'll try. When?'

'Soon. While there's still air enough. You go first. I'll be behind you.'

It was better for him that way. The first one through would have an easier passage, unhampered by the leader's thrusting feet. And if he gave up there was the hope that
10 she might have the strength to push him through. For a second she wondered how she would cope if the passage narrowed and his inert body blocked her escape. But she put the thought away from her. He was now less strong than she; weakened by cold and terror. He must go first. The water was now so high that only a fragile ribbon of light marked the exit. Its beam lay pale as milk on the dark surface. With the next wave that,
15 too, would go and they would be trapped in utter darkness with nothing to point the way out. She tugged off her waterlogged jersey. They let go of the ladder, joined hands, and paddled to the middle of the cave where the roof was highest, then turned on their backs and gulped in their long last lungfuls of air. The rock face almost scraped Cordelia's forehead. Water, cool and sweet, fell on her tongue like the last taste of life.
20 She whispered, 'Now!' and he let go of her hand without hesitation and slid under the surface. She took her final gulp of air, twisted and dived.

She knew that she was swimming for her life, and that was almost all she knew. It had been a moment for action not for thought and she was unprepared for the darkness, the icy terror, the strength of the inflowing tide. She could hear nothing but a
25 pounding in her ears, feel nothing but the pain above her heart and the black tide against which she fought like a desperate and cornered beast. The sea was death and she struggled against it with all she could muster of life and youth and hope. Time had no reality. It could have been minutes, even hours, that passage through hell, yet it must have been counted in seconds. She wasn't aware of the thrashing body in front of her.
30 She had forgotten Simon, forgotten Ambrose, forgotten even the fear of dying in the struggle not to die. And then, when the pain was too great, her lungs bursting, she saw the water above her lighten, become translucent, gentler, warm as blood and she thrust herself upward to the air, the open sea and the stars.

Notes *swim for it:* take a chance by swimming	*paddled:* (here) swam with their hands
unhampered: not obstructed, not held up	*gulped in:* breathed in deeply
thrusting: pushing hard	*twisted:* turned her body quickly
cope: manage	*pounding:* a beating noise
inert: lifeless, unmoving	*cornered:* with no way out
fragile: (here) lasting only a short time	*muster:* gather together
utter: complete	*thrashing:* swimming wildly
waterlogged: soaked with water, therefore very heavy	*translucent:* with light showing through it

Comprehension

The author

Decide whether these statements are true (**T**) or false (**F**).

1 Phyllis Dorothy White is the real name of P. D. James.

2 She was educated at Oxford High School.

3 She was an administrator for a regional crime board.

4 She has used her work experiences in her writing.

5 She has her own programme on television.

The text

A Write the opposites of these words and phrases from the text.

1	easier (line 8)	7	first (line 13)
2	gave up (line 9)	8	high (line 13)
3	strength (line 10)	9	light (line 13)
4	narrowed (line 11)	10	let go of (line 16)
5	weakened (line 12)	11	sweet (line 19)
6	cold (line 12)	12	life (line 22)

B Answer these questions.

1 What does Cordelia suggest as a way of escaping? Read the whole text and explain her plan in detail.

2 Why does Simon want to stay in the underground room?

3 Why do they have to escape very soon?

4 Why should Simon go first?

5 What are Cordelia's doubts about her escape plan?

6 How can they see the way out of the underground room?

7 Why does she take off her jersey?

8 Why do they 'paddle to the middle of the cave' (line 17)?

9 What is Cordelia thinking about as she swims?

10 What makes her swim so difficult?

11 Why is there a 'pain above her heart' (line 25)?

12 What is it that she is fighting against?

13 Do we know how long her swim lasts?

14 How do we know that she succeeds in escaping, and does not drown?

Discussion

1 'She fought like a desperate and cornered beast' (line 26). Why does the author use this language to describe Cordelia's escape? What other words or expressions are used to show us how dangerous it is, and how close Cordelia is to death? Is this an exciting text to read? If so, why?

2 How do you feel about the sea? Do you think it is often dangerous? How do you think people who make their living from the sea, like fishermen, feel about it?

3 Imagine how the story continues. What do you think has happened to Simon? Does Cordelia try to go back to the island, or to the mainland? How does she get there? Does she tell the police everything she knows?

Role-play

Student A: You and a friend (Student B) are planning a sailing trip in a borrowed boat this weekend. Neither of you has sailed before, but you think sailing looks very easy. You certainly haven't got enough money to hire any expensive equipment, like life-jackets. Anyway, you hate making complicated preparations for outings.

Student B: You think it's very important to have all the right safety equipment with you, in case something goes wrong. You also want to ask another friend, who is an experienced sailor, to come with you and be in charge of the boat. Try to explain to Student A how dangerous the sea can be.

Extension

Vocabulary

A '(They) gulped in their long last lungfuls of air' (line 18). Complete the sentences with the correct forms of these verbs: *chew gulp sip suck swallow taste.*

1 Don't .... your food. It's bad for your digestion.
2 He was so thirsty he .... the last drop of juice out of the orange.
3 If the coffee's too hot, just .... it.
4 Can you .... this pill with some water? It'll make you feel better.
5 The meat was so tough that I had to .... it for ages.
6 She .... the soup to see if it needed more salt.

B Use these words to complete the sentences: *handful armful tablespoonful mouthful lungful.*

1 He took a(n) .... of the pizza and said it was delicious.

2 Just add two .... s of flour as you beat the mixture.
3 Those children of hers are a real ....! She just can't control them!
4 As soon as he came out of the warm smoky room into the street, he breathed in .... s of the cold clear night air.
5 She staggered upstairs carrying .... s of books.

Grammar

'Time had no reality' (line 27). Decide whether articles are needed in the following sentences, and add *a, an* or *the* where necessary.

1 She looked at me without .... hope in her eyes.
2 .... women in my office all go to .... regular keep-fit classes.
3 He often drinks .... mineral water at .... lunch-time.
4 I'm sorry, but .... life is like that.
5 It's still true that .... men are more likely to earn a high salary than .... women.
6 .... love makes .... world go round.
7 Did you give me back .... money I lent you?
8 Investigations have begun into .... death of .... tourist on .... Scottish island of Mull.
9 We all have to face .... death sometime.
10 His flat is in .... Western Road, very near .... town centre.

Composition (120 – 180 words)

Write a letter to a friend of yours, telling him/her about a frightening incident recently, when you nearly drowned. Luckily you were rescued just in time. Explain what happened and describe your feelings.

FURTHER DISCUSSION

1 Compare Units 1 and 2. How are Crusoe's and Gulliver's experiences similar, and how are they different? What is the connection between these units and Unit 27?

2 Look at Units 3 and 6. In Unit 3 Mrs Bennet is hoping to arrange weddings for her daughters; in Unit 6 Rebecca is making her own plans to catch a husband. What do you think both these writers are trying to do? Which do you find more amusing?

3 In both Units 9 and 23 a man proposes marriage to a woman. How different are the characters of the men and women involved? Do you think both couples will be happy?

4 Look at Units 11 and 13. In both these units a romance begins with a conversation. Do the men have different reasons for starting the conversation? And how different or similar are the two girls?

5 Units 26 and 29 both deal with death. How do the two writers differ in their treatment of it?

6 Units 19 and 30 are both about women trying to escape. Explain what they are trying to escape from in the two texts, and show how the writers describe the women's feelings.

7 Can you find similarities between the descriptions of the two men in Units 20 and 22? How are their daily routines different from each other?

8 The action in several of the texts takes place at night. Look at Units 5, 10, 14 and 17, and say how the darkness or moonlight helps to create the atmosphere, and sometimes even brings about a development in the story.

9 Which text did you find most interesting or enjoyable, and why?

10 Choose a unit and prepare a talk to present the text to the rest of your class. Explain the reasons for your choice.

INDEX TO EXERCISES

Numbers are unit numbers.

KEY

1 DANIEL DEFOE

The author

1b 2c 3b

The text

A 1g 2c 3b 4e 5a 6d 7f

B 1 My next task/The next thing I had to do was to
2 I did not yet know/I had no idea
3 no more than a mile/less than a mile
4 I went exploring
5 but did not know what kind they were
6 When I returned/On my way back
7 each bird calling in its usual way

C 1 To keep them safe.
2 To explore, to get a good view of where he is.
3 In case he meets wild animals, or unfriendly people; perhaps also to shoot animals or birds for food.
4 Very depressed.
5 Because they are different from the birds in England/Europe.
6 Because the birds fly up in such confusion, he thinks they have never heard such a loud noise before. The island is completely wild and unexplored.
7 He is relieved that the island appears to be uninhabited.
8 He is afraid of being attacked and eaten by a wild animal.
9 The animals may be too frightened of him to attack, or there may be no wild animals on the island.
10 He uses the chests and boards he brought from the ship.

Grammar

A 1 He asked when the banks closed.
2 He asked where they came from.
3 He asked if/whether I/we spoke Italian.
4 He asked if/whether I/we had gone/been there the day before/the previous day.
5 He asked how long I/we had been working there.
6 He asked if/whether I/we had been there before.
7 He asked how long they would be staying.
8 He asked if/whether I/we could go there the next day/the following day/the day after.
9 He asked if/whether I was/we were ready yet.
10 He asked who I was/we were.

B 1 the
2 –,–
3 the, the
4 a, a
5 –
6 the, the
7 –
8 an, an, –
9 the
10 a, a, the, the, the

Negative adjectives

1 unintelligent
2 illegible
3 impractical
4 illiterate

5 impatient
6 impolite
7 unfit
8 irresponsible
9 uncomfortable
10 immature
11 irrational
12 inconvenient
13 illogical
14 impossible
15 unfair
16 insecure

---

2 JONATHAN SWIFT

The author

1 He was an English diplomat's secretary.
2 Correct.
3 He became a church administrator and writer.
4 He was a Protestant.
5 He founded a hospital for the poor.
6 Correct.
7 His life was full of disappointments.
8 He became one of the greatest satirical writers in English.

The text

A 1f 2a 3d 4g 5h 6b 7c 8e

B 1 as I calculated/guessed
2 more than/over nine hours
3 could not move
4 the light hurt my eyes
5 While this was happening
6 I was extremely surprised
7 I found out how they had tied me (up)
8 trying hard to free myself
9 which hurt me very much
10 after it finished/stopped

C 1 Because he is exhausted after the shipwreck.
2 Because he is tied down to the ground.
3 A small man, less than six inches tall, with a bow and arrow.
4 They are frightened, and run away.
5 'How wonderful/strange!' 'Shoot your arrows!'
6 By pulling at the ropes.
7 They run away again, and then shoot arrows at him.
8 He covers his face with his left hand.

Word-building

1 embarrassment
2 darkness
3 loneliness
4 explanation
5 education
6 promotion
7 ability
8 movement
9 sincerity
10 argument
11 security
12 laziness
13 intelligence
14 performance
15 appearance
16 interference
17 popularity
18 entrance

Vocabulary and idioms

1 leg	5 breast	9 arm
2 tongue	6 neck	10 heart
3 foot	7 finger	
4 shoulder	8 feet	

Grammar

A 1 It was such a beautiful day that we decided to have a picnic in the park.
2 There's so much/such a lot of furniture in their lounge that it's difficult to move around.
3 He did so little work that he failed his exams.
4 It was such terrible news that we all felt depressed.
5 They had such a wonderful holiday that they decided to go back to the Algarve next year.
6 There were so few spectators that the match was postponed.
7 Mark's boss was so impressed with his work that he gave Mark a pay rise.
8 The recipe was so complicated that Liz couldn't follow it.

3 JANE AUSTEN

The author

1F 2T 3T 4F 5F

The text

A 1 his lady (line 1)
2 returned (line 4)
3 tiresome (line 20)
4 design (line 22)
5 likely (line 23)
6 occasion (line 25)
7 handsome (line 26)
8 grown up (line 29)
9 give over (line 30)
10 hearty (line 40)

B 1 I don't mind hearing it
2 This gave her enough encouragement to continue
3 he made an agreement with Mr Morris
4 he will move into/be entitled to live in the house
5 What do you mean?
6 I see no reason for doing that
7 I do not claim to be beautiful now
8 when he comes/moves into the area
9 only because of that/for that reason
10 make a special recommendation

C 1a Mr Morris b Mrs Long c Lizzy d Sir William and Lady Lucas
2 Because he is a wealthy young bachelor, and she has several unmarried daughters.
3 He is just pretending, because he disapproves of his wife's matchmaking.
4 No, he isn't serious, but Mrs Bennet takes him seriously.
5 No, he isn't. He enjoys teasing his wife.

6 Mrs Bennet is rather superficial, only interested in appearances and in marrying off her daughters to rich men. She has no sense of humour. Mr Bennet does not want to be involved in her plans: he regards her with ironic detachment.

Grammar

A 1 get back
2 calls
3 have been
4 starts
5 send/have sent
6 leave
7 receive
8 dismiss
9 has saved up

B 1 monotonously
2 nearly
3 seldom
4 well
5 comfortably
6 soon
7 Suddenly
8 Unfortunately

4 EMILY BRONTË

The author

1 Correct.
2 She was the fifth of six children.
3 She seldom went abroad.
4 She only wrote one novel.
5 She was closest to her sister Anne.
6 She had a short life.
7 She spent most of her childhood at home.
8 Correct.

The text

A 1 infected with an illness/to be avoided
2 I intend to/I feel like (being)
3 I insist on having it
4 the key
5 he got it back quickly
6 move away
7 Not paying any attention to/Ignoring this warning
8 trying her hardest/as hard as she could
9 she bit
10 he gave up/let her have the thing they were quarrelling about
11 before she had really got hold of it/got hold of it properly
12 if she had been able to fall

B 1g 2f 3c 4b 5h 6a 7e 8d

C 1 Because Nelly is standing waiting for her at the door.
2 Linton, Heathcliff's son.
3 To keep Nelly and Catherine inside.
4 He is giving Linton to Catherine as a husband.
5 'pushing me forward' (line 3), '(he) struck the table' (line 13), '... or I shall knock you down' (line 24), '(he) administered ... a shower of terrific slaps on both

sides of the head' (line 32), 'A touch on the chest silenced me' (line37).
6 Catherine and Linton.
7 Her mother, whom Heathcliff was in love with. Catherine's answer reminds Heathcliff of the woman he loved.
8 He threatened to knock Catherine down (line 24).
9 Nelly does not fully realize what is happening, and is a little afraid of Heathcliff.
10 Presumably because nobody has ever punished her like this or hit her before.

Vocabulary

A 1 tiny, small, big, huge, gigantic
2 dull, routine, interesting, fascinating
3 freezing, cold, cool, tepid, warm, hot, boiling
4 disgusting, tasteless, nice, tasty, delicious
5 miserable, unhappy, satisfied, happy, delighted, overjoyed
6 evil, wicked, bad, naughty, good, angelic

Grammar

1 to getting up
2 to seeing
3 on having
4 to doing
5 of listening
6 in applying for
7 of flying

Expressions

1 by hand.
2 the bill by credit card?
3 him by sight.
4 put the wrong letter in the envelope by mistake.
5 by chance/accident.
6 by car.
7 the speech by heart.

5 CHARLOTTE BRONTË

The author

1 She did not like her first boarding school.
2 She studied in Brussels and met a teacher there.
3 She fell in love with but did not marry him.
4 Correct.
5 She travelled in England and abroad.

The text

A 1d 2h 3c 4j 5b 6i 7f 8g 9a 10e

B 1 She hears a vague murmur.
2 Two o'clock in the morning.
3 She hears a hand brushing her bedroom door.
4 It seems so close to the keyhole of her door.
5 Because she hears footsteps going back up the stairs to the top of the house, where she met Grace Poole before.
6 There is a lighted candle just outside, and smoke in the air.

7 She sees the smoke coming from there.
8 She finds Mr Rochester asleep, with his bed on fire.

C 1f 2d 3a 4c 5b 6e

Grammar

1 I wish I hadn't bought that car.
2 I wish she hadn't married him.
3 I wish you had told me the truth.
4 I wish I'd never started smoking.
5 I wish you hadn't invited those awful people.
6 I wish I hadn't been so rude to him.
7 I wish you had given me that advice earlier.
8 I wish I hadn't moved to the village.

Vocabulary

A 1f (view) 2c (dessert) 3e (scream) 4d (disease) 5a (yell) 6b (story)

B 1 smoke 2 glow 3 blazing 4 light 5 ashes

6 WILLIAM THACKERAY

The author

1F 2T 3F 4F 5F 6T 7F 8F

The text

A 1 she said, completely truthfully
2 Amelia was very kind, and sympathetic to Rebecca's problems
3 why should she criticize her brother?
4 Miss Sharp would never have been so foolish as to make statements which could easily be proved lies
5 she is still only nineteen
6 not used to the technique/skill of telling lies
7 she decided to make this praiseworthy effort

B 1 affectionate (line 7)
2 precious (line 8)
3 absence (line 16)
4 scarcely (line 17)
5 checked herself (line 18)
6 income (line 22)
7 your sister-in-law (line 23)
8 tenderness (line 31)
9 queries (line 35)
10 a fortnight (line 37)

C 1 is an orphan.
2 richer
3 hardly notices her.
4 that Amelia had told her Joseph was not married.
5 that Rebecca loves little children.
6 try to persuade Joseph to propose to her.

Vocabulary

A 1e 2a 3c 4g 5h 6d 7f 8b

B 1 pocket-money 5 pension
2 deposit 6 tips
3 fine 7 grant
4 refund 8 salary

Grammar

1 He said (that) he was sorry he would not be there.
2 She accused her husband of taking/having taken her keys.
3 The policeman denied (that) the Cray brothers had had anything to do with it/said that the Cray brothers had had nothing to do with it.
4 The doctor apologized for having been unable to get there in time/The doctor said that unfortunately he hadn't been able/had been unable to get there in time.
5 The film star said (that) Tom had always been his/her friend.
6 Edward said (that) he thought Sue was in the library.
7 They said (that) they had to be home by 11.30/They insisted on being home by 11.30.
8 The woman said (that) the children never drank milk with their meals.
9 The sculptor said (that) he didn't know if/whether he could finish the work.
10 My mother said (that) she hoped he was looking after me.

7 CHARLES DICKENS

The author

1F 2F 3T 4T 5F

The text

A 1d 2a 3f 4b 5c 6e

B 1 a pretty large room (line 1)
2 less splendid than (line 8)
3 scattered about (line 9)
4 had but one shoe on (line 10)
5 had lost its lustre, was faded (line 17)
6 I would have cried out, if I could (line 26)
7 avoiding her eyes (line 32)
8 took note of the surrounding objects in detail (line 32)

C 1 At least seventy years old.
2 She is still wearing her wedding dress, although her wedding day was years ago: she can't forget what happened on that day.
3 He has never seen anyone like her before: she makes him think of death and decay.
4 She has become as thin as a skeleton, and lost her youth and beauty.
5 Seeing a waxwork statue of a dead person, and seeing a skeleton in the vault of a church.

6 That must have been the moment when she heard that her fiancé had decided not to marry her.

Vocabulary

A 1 A bridegroom is the man at a wedding who is getting married.
2 A bride is the woman at a wedding who is getting married.
3 A bridesmaid is a girl/woman who helps/supports the bride.
4 The best man is the man who helps/supports the bridegroom.
5 A honeymoon is a holiday for the married couple after the wedding.

B 1 meat 5 tools 9 furniture
2 vegetables 6 trees 10 dairy/milk
3 fish 7 flowers products
4 metals 8 fruit

C 1 glowing 2 glittered 3 gleam 4 shone 5 dazzled

Phrasal verbs

1 put you up.
2 put off our meeting until next week.
3 put up with your job at the moment.
4 put me off helping him.
5 put forward a suggestion.
6 central heating put in recently.
7 to put down a deposit.
8 put you through?

Grammar

1 had left 5 had not shaved
2 arrived, found 6 set off, phoned
3 hadn't seen 7 bumped, hadn't seen
4 hadn't done 8 had been/gone, bought

8 GEORGE ELIOT

The author

1 Mary Ann/Marian Evans. 4 Charles Dickens
2 1819. 5 *Middlemarch*
3 *Scenes of Clerical Life.* 6 1880.

The text

A 1a 2f 3i 4c 5e 6g 7d 8j 9h 10b

B 1 he took out his coins
2 an unusually good meal for him
3 happiness is like a very good wine
4 he had not seen correctly
5 he dropped the candle
6 being able to avoid the awful truth just for a moment
7 there was nothing on the table
8 he had already looked for them, but hadn't found them

C 1 After supper.
2 No. Eliot compares Silas's enjoyment of his gold to a wine-drinker's enjoyment of a very good wine with his meal.
3 In bags under the floor near his loom.
4 No.
5 Silas can't understand what's happening to him: it's as if he were drowning, and trying to touch firm ground, but there is no firm ground. He has to accept that the worst has happened.
6 He hopes he has put his gold somewhere else, and will find it.
7 In his bed, in the oven, in every corner.
8 His gold has been stolen.
9 He screams, then goes to his usual seat at the loom.
10 Because it is a real and reassuring part of his daily routine: at least this has not changed.

Vocabulary

1 marched   3 limping   5 stroll
2 staggered   4 skipped   6 trudged

Grammar

1 whose   4 which/that   7 who
2 who   5 whose   8 that
3 where   6 which/that

Confusing verbs

1 laid   5 lying   9 lain
2 lie   6 laid   10 lying
3 lay   7 lay
4 lied   8 lying

---

9 ELIZABETH GASKELL

The author

1 her aunt in Cheshire.
2 Manchester.
3 busy and happy.
4 she wanted to express her sadness at the death of her only son.
5 she wrote a biography of her.

The text

A 1 her father (now dead) wanted to give her my name
2 allowing him to do what he wanted
3 make people think badly of her
4 her life will be difficult enough anyway
5 reminded of his daughter Molly
6 to love her as much as your own daughter/as if she were your own daughter
7 it was too late to take back the words
8 that period of my life is finished

B 1 Cynthia is a short form of Hyacinth.
2 He is unwilling to get involved in such a personal conversation.
3 Possibly other young men who would have liked to marry her.
4 She implies that looking after a young daughter is a great responsibility, especially for a man. This makes Mr Gibson think of his motherless daughter Molly, and encourages him to think of marrying Mrs Kirkpatrick and gaining a stepmother for Molly.
5 A mother.
6 She appears rather insincere: she pretends to be affectionate towards Molly in order to encourage Mr Gibson to propose.
7 She thinks, 'Is he going to offer?' and 'she began to tremble in the suspense' (line 25).
8 Whether it was wise of him to propose to her.
9 She is so relieved not to have to work for her living any more.
10 Mrs Kirkpatrick is too formal, and she is known by her previous surname, Clare, in the family where she now works.
11 It is a painful reminder that she has been a governess, and she wants to forget that now.

Word-building

1 memory   5 surprising, surprise
2 pride   6 wisdom
3 doubtful, doubt   7 hesitation
4 lost, loss

Conjunctions

1 However   5 but
2 but   6 Although
3 Despite   7 despite
4 Although   8 However

Phrasal verbs

1 went off   5 went over/through
2 went down/up   6 go out
3 go with   7 went by/past
4 going on

---

10 WILKIE COLLINS

The author

1b 2a 3c 4b

The text

A 1c 2d 3f 4a 5b 6e

B 1 all the doors were locked
2 my feet made a noise on the stones
3 creep quickly and quietly

4 as I had intended
5 going back quickly
6 a younger, fitter person than me
7 waiting for the right moment to commit a crime
8 keen to find out where (the Diamond) was

C 1 Gabriel, the butler (the narrator), with the footman.
2 He intends to go outside for some fresh air.
3 The shadow of someone round the corner.
4 He's old and heavy, rather unfit.
5 At least two.
6 They hide among the trees and bushes, and escape over the fence.
7 Because Samuel is younger and fitter.
8 A bottle of ink.
9 Indians have recently been seen in the village, performing tricks with ink.
10 The Diamond, the Moonstone.

Similes

1d as deaf as a post
2f as good as gold
3h as old as the hills
4g as dry as dust
5e as fresh as a daisy
6c as poor as a church mouse
7b as easy as pie
8a as pretty as a picture

Grammar

A 1 If he had told the truth, I would have believed him.
2 If I had been able to speak Russian, they would have offered me the job.
3 If he had shown any compassion for his victims, he wouldn't have been given a life sentence.
4 If I had used my calculator, I wouldn't have got the sum wrong.
5 If the cottage hadn't been so far from/had been nearer the main road, they would have bought it.
6 If you had said you were sorry, I could/would have forgiven you.
7 If she had followed the recipe, the cake wouldn't have turned out badly.
8 If he had known how selfish she was, he might/would not have married her.
9 If I had tried acupuncture treatment, I might/would have been able to stop smoking.
10 If I had known (I was supposed to), I would have worn a suit to the office.

B 1 more comfortable
2 easier
3 richer
4 more difficult
5 happier
6 more intelligent
7 uglier
8 more flexible
9 slower
10 thinner
11 more modern
12 cleverer/more clever
13 heavier
14 more beautiful
15 friendlier/more friendly
16 better
17 more educational
18 worse
19 faster
20 farther/further

C 1 then
2 than
3 than
4 then
5 then
6 than
7 than

---

11 THOMAS HARDY

The author

1c 2a 3b

The text

A 1a 2c 3e 4b 5g 6d 7f

B 1 I'm not as clever as you
2 expressing my thoughts in words
3 I never was very intelligent
4 a light, unimportant conversation
5 pressing her lips together
6 only for a moment
7 did completely the opposite
8 someone who does not have strong/deep feelings

C 1 He doesn't need to know, as they probably won't meet again.
2 She might soon/could easily get married and take her husband's name.
3 She's a little embarrassed by his seriousness.
4 He doesn't want to appear to show his feelings too much.
5 Country girls, who use their hands for their work, usually have rough hands.

Vocabulary

1 blunt
2 rough
3 tough
4 nervous/unsure
5 loose
6 innocent
7 mean
8 quiet

Expressions

1c 2f 3d 4b 5a 6e

Punctuation

1 Where's the teachers' room, please? I want to see Mr Jones and Miss Green.
2 The mountain's not in Tibet: it's in Nepal.
3 Five oranges, please, and two apples.
4 The cat drank its milk.
5 He's a friend of John's, isn't he?
6 You shouldn't have taken his pens.
7 It's time we did some work in Michael's garden.
8 The students' bags were lying on the floor(,) where they'd left them.

Grammar

1 slowly
2 angrily
3 comfortably
4 fast

5 automatically   7 beautifully
6 well   8 hard

Prepositions

1 of   6 for   11 about
2 of   7 at   12 with
3 about   8 of   13 to
4 with   9 of   14 at
5 to   10 of

---

12 MARK TWAIN

The author

1 He only spent his childhood and youth in Hannibal.
2 He did not study journalism, but became a journalist.
3 He became famous for his satirical writing.
4 He married in 1870.
5 His later writing was beginning to show signs of pessimism.

The text

A 1e 2a 3b 4d 5h 6c 7i 8g 9j 10f

B 'the graces, the winning ways, and the rare promise' (line 13); 'their sweet, generous natures' (line 18); 'noble and beautiful', (line 19). faults and flaws' (line 16).

C 1 everybody there was touched/moved
   2 the boys should have been (and perhaps were) whipped for their wicked behaviour
   3 everybody in the church cried and wept together
   4 the priest stood without moving, astonished
   5 Huck's clothes were extremely dirty and ragged/torn
   6 trying to creep quietly, feeling embarrassed
   7 gave grateful, relieved cries
   8 Aunt Polly hugged and kissed him and spoke kindly to him

D 1 Their families think the boys are dead.
   2 They only remember the boys' good qualities, not their faults.
   3 Emotional, mournful, tearful, tragic.
   4 They are amazed and delighted.
   5 He is an orphan, so doesn't belong to any particular family.
   6 No, worse.

Vocabulary

1 delegates   5 staff
2 audience   6 viewers
3 jury   7 congregation
4 team   8 spectators

Animal expressions

1 dog   5 horse
2 worm   6 rat
3 cat   7 wolf
4 fish

Grammar

1 He was given a bicycle for his birthday by his father.
2 The flat next door is being painted.
3 A cure for the common cold has not been discovered yet.
4 It is said that you shouldn't eat too much salt/Too much salt shouldn't be eaten.
5 That house has not been lived in for years.
6 A lot of ice-cream is consumed in hot weather.
7 You will be met at the airport.
8 The bypass is going to be built as planned.

---

13 HENRY JAMES

The author

1 New York, London, Paris and Geneva.
2 American magazines.
3 many famous literary figures.
4 Britain/England.
5 short stories.
6 character description ... plot.
7 mastery of the psychological novel.

The text

A 1b 2c 3b 4a

B 1 She is a shy, reserved girl.
   2 Mr Townsend takes charge of the conversation.
   3 No. He seems rather too complimentary. He is probably trying to impress Catherine.
   4 He doesn't appear to expect an answer.
   5 He seems different from other men, the best-looking man she has ever seen.
   6 She lets him put his arm round her waist.
   7 She gets hot, and fans herself.
   8 Because she is falling in love with Mr Townsend.
   9 It only has room for two people.
   10 Nothing, apart from looking at him and smiling.
   11 Relaxed, happy, admiring.
   12 He has more delicate features, he is more handsome.

Grammar

1 turning   6 to get
2 talking   7 to inform
3 to lock   8 studying
4 to send   9 to buy
5 leaving/having left   10 bumping

Relative pronouns

1	What	6	which
2	which	7	what
3	which	8	which
4	that	9	what
5	what	10	that/which

14 ROBERT LOUIS STEVENSON

The author

1 Correct.
2 He travelled for his health.
3 He married an American woman.
4 He died in Samoa.
5 Correct.
6 He is most famous for *Treasure Island*.

The text

A 1d 2a 3b 4c 5f 6g 7h 8e

B 1 I'll take what I am owed and nothing more
2 and I don't know what else
3 in no particular order
4 that frightened me terribly
5 inside and outside
6 let's leave now
7 get us involved in a very dangerous situation
8 quite a long way away
9 to settle the debt, make it fair
10 were escaping as fast as possible

C 1 Silver, trinkets, a boat-cloak, a bundle tied up in oilcloth, and a canvas bag.
2 It is more than the pirate captain owes her.
3 They are in different values and currencies.
4 The guineas.
5 The tapping of the blind man's stick on the road.
6 He knows the pirates are coming back, and they may be violent.
7 Not taking more than she is owed.
8 When they hear a whistle and realize the pirates are on their way back.
9 Some coins and the oilcloth bundle.
10 They can't be seen as they leave the inn.
11 The fog is lifting and they will soon be in moonlight. Also, one of the people coming towards them has a lantern.
12 The pirates.

Word-building

1	lengthen	5	loosen	9	strengthen
2	straighten	6	widen	10	shorten
3	flatten	7	blacken	11	darken
4	deepen	8	redden	12	tighten

Expressions

1	at first sight	4	at last	7	at least
2	at once	5	at night	8	at most
3	at times	6	at a glance		

Grammar

1 To my horror I saw that one of the windows was broken.
2 To her delight she discovered she had passed all her exams.
3 To their surprise they sold their house at a profit.
4 To our amazement we didn't have to pay for the theatre tickets.
5 To my astonishment (I saw that) he had aged considerably since our last meeting.
6 To her relief her children returned home safe and sound.

15 JEROME K. JEROME

The author

1 east London.
2 jobs/occupations.
3 a humorous magazine called *The Idler*.
4 *Three Men in a Boat*.
5 several other books, and articles and plays.

The text

A 1 We spent less than five seconds getting it
2 This seemed an important point/a reasonable objection
3 We decided to reject the idea that Harris had been taken to heaven
4 a little sadly
5 horrified, terrified
6 he had fallen over, taking the pie with him

B 1 For Harris to cut the pie, and give them some.
2 To get a spoon from the picnic hamper.
3 George and the narrator were between Harris and the river.
4 The pie wouldn't have been taken as well.
5 Perhaps the angels who might have taken Harris up to heaven!
6 He was looking forward to eating the pie.
7 They can only see his head, and are not sure whether he is dead or alive.
8 He thinks it is all their fault.
9 He fell backwards into a small dip in the ground.
10 'The end of the world has come.'

Grammar

A 1 couldn't have got the job
2 couldn't have caused
3 couldn't have passed on the message
4 couldn't have translated that letter
5 couldn't have seen the Queen in London yesterday

B 1 We bought all our books yesterday.
2 Oh, no! I've lost my keys!
3 Have you ever won a prize?
4 I wrote ten letters before lunch yesterday.
5 They first came to England in 1988.
6 I've seen several interesting new films lately.
7 It's the first time she's made a speech in public.
8 They got married five years ago.
9 He hasn't done much work up to now.
10 The last time I saw him was when he visited me in Edinburgh.

C 1 the most comfortable
2 the best
3 the worst
4 the oldest
5 the furthest/farthest
6 the lightest
7 the most convenient
8 the most tired
9 the biggest
10 the most modern
11 the heaviest
12 the gentlest

Vocabulary

1 gazed
2 glimpse
3 Peering
4 glared
5 glanced
6 peeped
7 stare

Vocabulary

A 1c 2g 3a 4f 5j 6i 7b 8e 9h 10d

B 1 chef
2 greengrocer
3 dustman/ refuse collector
4 architect
5 actor/actress
6 optician
7 miner
8 sales assistant/ shop assistant
9 journalist/reporter
10 politician/Member of Parliament

Grammar

1 If you sent this portrait to the Grosvenor, you'd be/become famous.
2 If you weren't so proud, you'd exhibit the portrait.
3 If you were famous, people would be talking/talk about you.
4 If people were talking/talked about you, you'd get (a lot of) orders for new paintings.
5 If you painted/were painting more pictures, you'd be/become rich.
6 If you had (more) money, you could lead a more/very exciting and luxurious life.

16 OSCAR WILDE

The author

1F 2F 3T 4T 5T 6F

The text

A 1 extremely good-looking
2 not far away
3 made people imagine all sorts of reasons (for it)
4 What strange people you painters are/You painters are such strange people!
5 to become famous
6 Really, Basil!

B 1 The portrait he has painted of Dorian Gray.
2 He disappeared suddenly in strange circumstances.
3 It portrays an extremely handsome young man, and has been skilfully painted.
4 Pleasure in his artistic achievement, but also fear of something connected with the portrait.
5 He thinks the Academy is too big and interests only low-class people. He prefers seeing the people, not the pictures, at an art gallery.
6 Because it would be a good way of making himself famous, which all artists want to do.
7 He says he has put too much of himself into it.
8 He speaks 'languidly' (line 15), he is smoking a cigarette, and he 'stretched himself out on the divan and laughed' (line 33).
9 ... laugh at me.

17 SIR ARTHUR CONAN DOYLE

The author

1 He was born in Edinburgh.
2 He worked as a doctor for eight years.
3 Sherlock Holmes first appeared in *A Study in Scarlet*.
4 The public preferred his detective stories.
5 Correct.
6 He was knighted for his pamphlet about the Boer War.

The text

A 1g 2b 3e 4f 5a 6j 7h 8i 9d 10c

B 1 I think it would be a good idea
2 we went back the way we had come, followed by the fog
3 It's absolutely necessary/Whatever happens
4 put his ear to the ground
5 from the centre of the fog-bank
6 his mouth opened
7 shouted with fear
8 unable to think
9 a burning look
10 madness/a sick mind

C 1 The thick fog.
2 The top part of the house.
3 That the fog will cover the path very soon, and they won't be able to see.
4 So that they can wait on higher ground, out of the fog.

5 Sir Henry and, possibly, the hound.
6 Holmes.
7 He is delighted because he is about to face the hound.
8 He is so frightened.
9 He is too shocked by the hound's appearance to react.
10 A huge ghostly black dog, with its head and mouth giving off flames.

Vocabulary

A 1 buzzed   4 snapped   7 rustle
   2 crack   5 crash   8 splashing
   3 creaked   6 whizzed

B 1 awful   3 terrible   5 lovely
   2 horible   4 marvellous   6 wonderful

Grammar

1 I'll let you know if I change my mind.
2 Margaret will probably get the job if she sends in an/the application form.
3 If we have time, we'll stop for lunch on the way.
4 I'll give you a lift if you're in a hurry.
5 If you aren't careful, you'll have an accident.
6 If I can repair my car, I'll be able to use it tomorrow.
7 If he doesn't invite me to the/his party, I won't go.
8 My nephew will buy a/the mountain bike if he saves up enough money.
9 You can borrow my computer if yours breaks down.
10 Unless you go now, you'll be too late.

18 JOSEPH CONRAD

The author

1 the Polish Ukraine.
2 involved in revolutionary politics.
3 into exile in Russia.
4 looked after him when his father died.
5 reading English adventure stories.
6 had never heard English spoken.
7 England.
8 were the basis for much of his writing.

The text

A 1 serious, worried
   2 a good idea
   3 In addition
   4 as it was getting dark
   5 extremely cross
   6 we had to be careful
   7 stopped the ship
   8 nothing moved on the banks, there was silence
   9 huge, very large
   10 the noise of the chain, not clearly heard

B 1 He is keen to meet Kurtz.
   2 It is dangerous to take a ship through this part of the river, and it would be more dangerous in the dark.
   3 There may be rocks just under the water, or strong currents, or crocodiles.
   4 A local official who knows about conditions here.
   5 It is a steam ship, which uses wood as fuel.
   6 On the ship, in the middle of the river.
   7 It is strangely silent and unmoving.
   8 At first there is a thick white fog, which lifts and then comes down again. It is very warm and humid.
   9 They hear a loud, sad cry.
   10 It is so unexpected.
   11 As if nothing exists outside the ship.

Easily confused words

1 sensitive   4 expecting   7 worthless
2 likeable   5 fun   8 left
3 advice   6 effect

Grammar

1 to send   4 stay up   7 feel
2 wear   5 to finish   8 go
3 to admit   6 to come

19 E. M. FORSTER

The author

1 he was dominated by the women in his family.
2 made friends and enjoyed the stimulating atmosphere.
3 he did not need to earn money.
4 *A Passage to India*.
5 all his major novels have been filmed.

The text

A 1f 2d 3b 4c 5g 6e 7h 8a

B 1 it was possible to leave the house unnoticed
   2 there was a loud grating noise as she turned the key
   3 thinking she was a countrywoman
   4 there was just one large cypress tree, which broke the regularity of the circle of olive trees
   5 it had reached her
   6 was not loud enough to be heard
   7 if only he would turn round, just for a moment
   8 without trying any more/without making any more effort

C 1 Because she wants freedom, peace and a little exercise.
   2 She takes the key to the terrace door from Gino's suit pocket.
   3 Because she is becoming deaf.
   4 She is worried that someone might see her from the house, or might notice her absence.
   5 Like pillars of silver and black, and cliffs of pearl.

6 Because she is sentimental, and this place brings back memories of their early, happier relationship.
7 To Empoli, and eventually to England.
8 She changes her mind because she suddenly realizes how much she wants to get away from Italy.
9 Because her voice isn't loud enough, and he has begun to sing.
10 She feels as if she can no longer stay with Gino, and that her only hope is to take this opportunity to escape.
11 She tries to take a short cut, running across rough ground to meet the coach further on along the road.
12 The coach.
13 She is exhausted and upset.
14 Gino will be angry because she left the house without telling him.
15 She sees the house as a prison and feels she is going 'back to captivity' (line 40).

Phrasal verbs

1 turn off
2 turn back
3 turned away
4 turned up
5 turned down
6 turned out
7 turns to

Conjunctions

1 As
2 till
3 for/as
4 before
5 When
6 while
7 but

Relative pronouns

1 He gave me the money I had asked him for.
2 She resigned her job, which I thought was a mistake.
3 That's the house where Charles Dickens was born.
4 I ordered the book you recommended me to read.
5 He's the official you spoke to yesterday.
6 The interviewing panel appointed the applicant who was the last to be interviewed.
7 I went to collect the post, which was lying on the front doormat.

20   D. H. LAWRENCE

The author

1c 2d 3b 4d

The text

A 1 make his wife get up early
  2 alone/on his own
  3 as much of it as he could
  4 it was what he was used to in the coal-mine
  5 I've brought you a cup of tea, (my) dear

B 1 He makes his own breakfast.
  2 She stays in bed, sleeping or enjoying being alone.
  3 Very quiet and peaceful.

4 Because it's the only place where there is a fire, and his clothes are left there to warm.
5 To make it burn better, so that the kettle will boil.
6 Grilled bacon on a thick slice of bread, and a cup of tea.
7 No. They use a newspaper instead of a cloth.
8 He enjoys it, because his family are not there to criticize him and his eating habits.
9 His clasp-knife.
10 He puts rugs against the bottoms of the doors to keep the cold air out; and he sits close to the fire, with his back against the warm wall of the fireplace.
11 He has not learnt to read well.
12 Because the darkness/low light is what he has become used to in the mine.
13 Two thick slices of bread and butter, and a tin bottle of cold tea without milk or sugar.
14 He only remembers to do it sometimes.

Grammar

1 needn't
2 mustn't
3 mustn't
4 needn't
5 needn't
6 mustn't
7 needn't
8 mustn't

Vocabulary

1 jar
2 packet
3 tube
4 carton
5 box
6 chunk
7 bar
8 slice

Confusing verbs

1 raised
2 risen
3 rose
4 raise
5 raised
6 rise

21   ERNEST HEMINGWAY

The author

1 World War I.
2 American.
3 The Republicans.
4 1954.
5 Deep-sea fishing.
6 He committed suicide by shooting himself.

The text

A 1c 2e 3h 4b 6g 7a 8f

B 1 Because it is very cold at night.
  2 She and her husband own the guest-house: she comes in to shut the windows and light the stove.
  3 In bed.
  4 In order not to slip on the icy roads.
  5 An island with two trees.
  6 The plain of the Rhone Valley, two ranges of mountains, and the Dent du Midi: France.
  7 The mountain called the Dent du Midi. Because it is so high.

8 In a small living-room upstairs.
9 Reading and playing cards.
10 Yes. Mr and Mrs Guttingen 'were very happy together too' (line 34), so Catherine and Frederic must be happy.

C 1 Mrs Guttingen came in three times in the morning, first to close the windows and light the stove, next to bring wood for the fire and hot water for washing, and then to bring in breakfast.
2 From the chalet, you could walk either up the mountain, down the mountain, or through the pine forest.
3 Further up the valley there was the Dent du Midi, which dominated the valley/which was in France.
4 Sometimes it was sunny enough for the young couple to eat lunch on the porch, but most of the time they ate indoors/upstairs.
5 Mr and Mrs Guttingen's son did not live with them.

Grammar

1 Coming into the room unexpectedly, I found Tim reading my letter.
2 Arriving late for work, she discovered the boss waiting by her desk.
3 Feeling exhausted after his long day, he decided not to cook a meal.
4 Not understanding his question, I couldn't give him an answer.
5 Not knowing what else to do, she rang the police for help.

Vocabulary

A 1 chambermaid 3 waiter/waitress 5 manager
   2 porter   4 chef   6 receptionist

B 1 roared   4 snapped   7 crashed
   2 hissed   5 crunched
   3 whistled 6 banged

---

22 GEORGE ORWELL

The author

1 In Bengal, India.
2 Because he disapproved of colonialism.
3 He could not make enough money to live on.
4 The Spanish Civil War.
5 *Animal Farm*.
6 Pessimistic.

The text

A 1 Rejected by society, homeless, unemployed and very poor
   2 I want to describe him
   3 the only thing left which made the trousers wearable/the only remaining sign or reminder of the social position he once had

4 he would prefer to be hit than to hit someone himself
5 he was in the armed forces for two years, fighting for his country
6 he had learnt all the habits that tramps have
7 he made me have some of the sandwiches he had found
8 He did not want to commit any crimes
9 Somebody could steal that bottle, couldn't they?
10 We'd better leave it

B 1 He was tallish, about 35 years old, with fair hair going grizzled (grey) and watery blue eyes. His cheeks were thin and his skin looked greyish. He was dressed in a tweed shooting-jacket and a pair of very old evening trousers.
2 Because of his poor diet (bread and margarine).
3 He wants to appear respectable, to be able to shave, and brush his shoes.
4 His birth certificate and other identification documents.
5 The way he walks and hunches his shoulders identifies him as a tramp.
6 Because he lost his job.
7 Looking constantly at the pavements for useful things people have dropped, e.g. a cigarette-end or sandwiches; trying automatic machines for coins.
8 Because it is against his principles/he thinks it is wrong to steal.

Grammar

1 I didn't see anybody.
2 She doesn't really love him, does she?
3 I'm not going to tell the truth.
4 They were my friends, all of them.
5 He didn't do it.
6 She doesn't come here any more.
7 He certainly isn't leaving.
8 Have you been there before?

Expressions

1 out of breath   4 out of date   7 out of stock
2 out of sight   5 out of pocket   8 out of print
3 out of reach   6 out of control

Vocabulary

1 honest   3 selfish   5 reliable
2 generous 4 embarrassed   6 proud

---

23 DAPHNE DU MAURIER

The author

1 her to play cricket.
2 were classic boys' adventure stories.

3 was a well-known writer and illustrator.
4 types of stories/books.
5 was Cornwall.

The text

A 1 I'm behaving badly to you
2 You would feel we were doing things correctly/you were getting what you expected
3 what a pity
4 looking out to see what the weather was like
5 I could not control my imagination then
6 always lots of people
7 on the edge of a crowd
8 you are so good at being Mrs de Winter

B 1 'I also like new library books ...', 'The only difference is that ...'
2 We ought to be in a conservatory ...', 'And I should make violent love ...'
3 'Never mind, I'll take you to Venice ...', 'But we won't stay too long, because ...'
4 'We would be in a crowd of people ...', 'I considered my name ...'
5 'I heard myself talking on the telephone ...', 'Everyone looked towards me ...'

C 1 Because at first she isn't sure whether it's a job or marriage that he's offering.
2 When he says he wants to show her Manderley.
3 When she was a child, she happened to buy a picture postcard of Manderley. She now sees this as a premonition of her future role as mistress of the house.
4 He is eating his tangerine and watching her.
5 The rest of the tangerine is sour, and he advises her not to eat it.

Grammar

A 1 does she   6 will you
2 had you   7 didn't he
3 had she   8 aren't I
4 wouldn't they   9 will we
5 shall we   10 has she

B 1 live, am living   6 appears
2 is studying   7 eats
3 visit   8 tastes
4 am trying   9 is just parking
5 has   10 hates

Expressions

1 fish and chips   6 bread and butter
2 ladies and gentlemen   7 in and out
3 upstairs and downstairs 8 men and women
4 black and white   9 bed and breakfast
5 to and fro   10 backwards and forwards

24 EVELYN WAUGH

The author

1F 2F 3T 4F 5F 6F

The text

A 1f 2c 3d 4h 5a 6e 7g 8b

B 1 in a relaxed way
2 By using the money for my first-class ticket, we can both travel third-class
3 with a large number of small bundles (food or clothes rolled up)
4 looking as if they would obey any official orders quietly
5 going back (to their ships) after a holiday
6 We did not sleep well, but kept waking up
7 all our money except for a few francs (French currency)
8 getting in and getting out at each station, moving in waves

C 1 Because Charles had met Sebastian at Oxford, in what now seems like a separate existence.
2 His home, Brideshead.
3 Because Sebastian's parents are separated, his father provides a certain amount of money for his son through his lawyers.
4 'The long, cheap sea-crossing', 'sitting all night on deck', 'to Paris, on wooden seats', 'the slow train south, again the wooden seats', 'a carriage full of the poor'.
5 They shave and have a bath at a hotel, have lunch at a restaurant, wander around the shops and sit in a café, waiting for their train.
6 Because they can't afford sleepers, and are sitting on wooden seats; it is a slow train which stops and starts; once they have to change trains in the night.
7 They are crossing an international border.
8 By describing the difference in scenery, the different type of people ('of Southern grace and gaiety'), and pointing out the Southern food, smells and heat.
9 Because Sebastian should have been travelling first class in a sleeper, which is only available on the express.
10 Sebastian's father, Lord Marchmain.
11 By gondola.
12 Completely new, exciting, memorable.

Vocabulary

1c 2d 3f 4a 5b 6e

1 giggled   3 grinning   5 smirking
2 chuckled   4 cackled   6 guffawed

Grammar

1A 2C 3B 4C 5D 6B 7C 8F 9E 10B

25 GRAHAM GREENE

The author

1b 2c 3d 4a

The text

1 He knows she does not want him to discuss the 'accident' and reveal his information, which might be dangerous for him.
2 No, he heard it, and immediately looked out of the window.
3 A vehicle knocked down a pedestrian.
4 He saw three people carrying the body into the house.
5 He says it's better not to get involved, his office can't give him time off to give evidence, and he wasn't an eye-witness anyway. In fact he's afraid of what might happen to him if he gives evidence.
6 He works at the mortuary and can easily tell when a person is dead.
7 The other witnesses.
8 The doctor himself.
9 He says Koch should have given evidence.
10 Three, according to Koch.
11 Three men and the driver.
12 Martins has previously heard that there were two men and the driver: now Koch says it was three and the driver. Martins thinks he may have found a 'crack' in the wall of lies around the death of Harry Lime, and hopes he may be able to discover the truth.
13 One man wore a toupee (a wig), and the other two were ordinary-looking, of medium height and build.
14 He is not used to observing the living, only the dead.
15 He did not want to be identified as a witness.
16 The other witnesses told him there were only two men carrying the body, so Martins wants to know who the third man was.

Vocabulary

A 1 jury, verdict
2 accused, sentence
3 acquitted
4 prosecuted, fine
5 lawyer, statement

B 1 nosed
2 thumb
3 toe
4 elbowed
5 fingered
6 eyed
7 headed
8 handed

Word-building

1 childhood
2 relationship
3 kingdom
4 neighbourhood
5 friendship
6 parenthood

26 JOHN WYNDHAM

The author

1 was a barrister.
2 following several different careers first.
3 reading science fiction by H. G. Wells and Jules Verne.
4 his work science fiction.
5 published/wrote short stories.

The text

A 1 Her family have all died and she has nobody to look after her.
2 She's frightened and unhappy, and worried about Tommy.
3 He does not feel lonely any more, because he wants to help her.
4 They are probably brother and sister.
5 A triffid.
6 She hates it.
7 The triffid stung him.
8 It would have attacked and killed Bill and the child.
9 It is difficult to kill: Bill has to shoot it twice.
10 He must have been attacked by a triffid, and must have killed it by shooting it twice.
11 Very sad.
12 They were probably attacked by the triffids, and are also dead.
13 Perhaps he hasn't had time, there have simply been too many to bury, or he hasn't felt strongly enough about anyone up to now.

B 1 looking around me to see if there were any triffids near: this had become automatic/an instinct
2 I no longer felt so terribly lonely
3 I realized there were more things and people to think about than just myself and my worries/I had been protecting myself from feeling too much, but now I started to feel something
4 I could see immediately
5 As I had done before, I shot the triffid a second time, to kill it

Vocabulary

1e 2g 3h 4j 5f 6i 7a 8c 9b 10d

Grammar

1 'll be able
2 'll come
3 is taking/is going to take
4 'll answer
5 passes/'ll pass
6 is going to run
7 'll be working
8 will have left

Conjunctions

1 Despite being ill/Despite the fact that she was ill/Despite her illness she kept on working.

2 Even though I didn't get the job, I don't regret applying for it.
3 Although she didn't tell him the news, he heard it from someone else.
4 In spite of the terrible weather that day/In spite of the fact that the weather was terrible that day, we still went for a swim.
5 I don't like him, but I must admit he's good at his job.

Phrasal verbs

1	up	3	out	5	through/over
2	for	4	round	6	after

27 WILLIAM GOLDING

The author

1 Near Newquay in Cornwall.
2 Oxford.
3 He served in the Royal Navy.
4 *Lord of the Flies.*
5 1983.
6 Man's tendency towards evil.

The text

A 1e 2d 3f 4a 5b 6c

B 1 You can certainly swim well
2 What's your father's job?/What does your father do?
3 he looked for something but couldn't find it
4 She owned/managed a shop selling sweets, chocolates etc
5 Piggy came out of the water
6 Piggy continued to make his points/say what he wanted to say
7 walking under the burning heat of the sun
8 he found the clothes he had taken off and thrown carelessly around

C 1 Because his father taught him when he was five.
2 He is embarrassed or sad because he has no father.
3 Presumably because his mother had remarried or gone away, and was unwilling/unable to look after him.
4 To show that, although he had no parents, he had other advantages.
5 'The heat of the morning' (line 13), 'enduring the sun's enmity' (line 34).
6 He thinks nobody will come to rescue them.
7 The people at the airport which their plane came from.
8 He is starting to cry.
9 He likes the feeling of putting clothes on, to keep the sun's heat off his skin.
10 It's nearby, in the shade and suitable for sitting on.

Vocabulary

B 1	say	4	whispered	7	scream
2	speak	5	chat	8	argue
3	mention	6	discuss		

Phrasal verbs

1	after	4	up	7	in
2	on	5	back	8	over
3	to	6	off		

28 GERALD DURRELL

The author

1d 2a 3a 4b

The text

A 1f 2b 3d 4e 5c 6a 7h 8g

B 1 acting in his usual generous and hospitable way
2 to travel to Corfu and stay in the Durrells' house
3 He had not realized that (the villa wasn't big enough)
4 I really don't understand why you are complaining so much
5 even if we don't have any guests at all
6 We can't all share rooms and sleep in temporary beds
7 to invite friends to stay
8 They are very nice people

C 1 Larry is spontaneous but rather thoughtless, not thinking what problems his actions will cause. The author is certainly laughing at him.
2 It is only just big enough for the family.
3 She assumes Larry's friends will be staying there.
4 He thinks they will be staying in the Durrells' villa.
5 She says there isn't enough room for everyone to sleep there.
6 His mother, brothers and sister could give up their beds to the visitors, and sleep elsewhere.
7 She doesn't like the idea of the family sleeping in the sitting-room or on the veranda 'like gipsies', and thinks it's too cold to sleep outside anyway.
8 'Really, Larry, you are the most annoying creature.'
9 He suggests moving to a larger villa.
10 He says he invited them to make life more interesting for his mother: in fact, he just wanted to be hospitable to his friends.

Grammar

A 1 I wish I could come to the ceremony.
2 I wish he didn't/wouldn't talk so much.
3 I wish I could speak Greek.
4 I wish I could go out/it would stop raining.
5 I wish he would make up his mind.
6 I wish you would do some work for a change.
7 I wish I had a car.
8 I wish she would phone me.

B furniture, meat, fruit, accommodation, news, advice, information, luggage

C	1	few	3	much	5	a few
	2	a lot of	4	little	6	a little

29 AGATHA CHRISTIE

The author

1 in Torquay/in Devon/in 1890.
2 Hercule Poirot and Miss Marple.
3 professor and famous archaeologist.
4 wrote many stage plays.
5 than those of any other writer except Shakespeare.

The text

A 1 began to go faster
2 moving a little ahead
3 sometimes you could see the passengers in the other train
4 seemed to be standing still
5 the woman died
6 it had completely disappeared
7 how would it help
8 so close to her
9 Sorry, what did you say?
10 he stopped in the middle of his sentence

B 1 remorselessly (line 12)   4 apologetically (line 35)
2 automatically (line 19)   5 tactfully (line 37)
3 doubtfully (line 28)

C 1 side by side.
2 on the other train.
3 appeared to be trying to kill a woman.
4 she wasn't sure it was the right thing to do/would be any use.
5 to believe her.
6 on some action being taken/that something must be done.

Grammar

1	Any	4	any	7	some
2	some	5	any	8	Some
3	any	6	No		

Spelling

1	stationery	3	plane	5	write
2	farther	4	dyed		

Phrasal verbs

1 broke down   5 broke out/have broken out
2 broke into   6 broke away
3 break off   7 broke down
4 broke up

30 P. D. JAMES

The author

1T 2F 3F 4T 5F

The text

A	1	more difficult	7	last
	2	continued/carried on	8	low
	3	weakness	9	dark/darkness
	4	widened	10	held on to/got hold of
	5	strengthened	11	bitter/sour
	6	heat/warmth	12	death

B 1 First Simon, then Cordelia will dive down to find the way out of the underground room, swim through the narrow passage towards the light, and then up to the surface of the open sea.
2 He thinks he is likely to drown and he doesn't want to die alone, so he'd prefer to stay there, with her.
3 The tide is still coming in, and soon there will be no air in the underground room, and no light to mark the exit.
4 He is weaker and more frightened, and it will be easier for the person who goes first. Also, if he can't continue, she might be able to push him through the passage.
5 She wonders what she would do if the passage became narrow and he collapsed, blocking her escape route.
6 Light is coming in from the exit, through the narrow passage.
7 It is wet, and will make her heavier.
8 The roof is at its highest there, so there is more air.
9 She is concentrating on trying to survive.
10 She did not expect the darkness, the cold, her fear, the strong tide.
11 She has to hold her breath for a long time.
12 The 'black tide' – the sea, darkness and death.
13 Probably a number of seconds rather than minutes.
14 We read that she comes out into the air and sees the stars.

Vocabulary

A	1	gulp	3	sip	5	chew
	2	sucked	4	swallow	6	tasted

B	1	mouthful	3	handful	5	armfuls
	2	tablespoonfuls	4	lungfuls		

Grammar

1	-/any	5	-, -	9	-
2	The, -	6	-, the	10	-, the
3	-, -	7	the		
4	-	8	the, a, the		